The Man from Nazareth

The Man from Nazareth

The Story of Jesus According to Matthew, Mark, and Luke

Mel Storm

Wipf & Stock Publishers
Eugene, Oregon

THE MAN FROM NAZARETH:
THE STORY OF JESUS ACCORDING TO MATTHEW, MARK, AND LUKE

Wipf & Stock Publishers
199 W. 8th Ave., Suite 3
Eugene, OR 97401

ISBN: 1-59752-606-1

Cataloging-in-Publication data:

Storm, Mel,

The Man from Nazareth / Mel Storm

p. cm.

Includes bibliographical references.

ISBN 1-59752-606-1 (alk. paper)

BR128 I54 2006

Manufactured in the U.S.A.

Contents

Introduction

In the history of Christianity, students of the gospel during the first millennium of Christianity generally sought to harmonize the material in the four gospels in order to produce a single, unified story of Jesus. But in recent years, such harmonization has been rejected in favor of a variety of approaches which respects the theological and literary integrity of each gospel. With this perspective, each gospel would be studied as an independent narrative of Jesus' life, written from a particular point of view. Thus instead of one unified story, we have four different stories. Consequently, some scholars have questioned the wisdom of a book or course on the life of Jesus. While the concerns of these scholars merit consideration, I believe it is still possible to write a book on the life of Jesus. Therefore, the objective of this book has been to survey the life of Jesus by: (1) generally following the chronology of Mark, while noting and explaining significant variations in Matthew and Luke; (2) inserting important material unique to either Matthew or Luke, particularly material on the sayings of Jesus; (3) presenting theological and literary explanations for variations over harmonistic explanations, thus respecting the integrity of each gospel; (4) seeking to establish literary and historical contexts for each gospel unit while also noting those places where the evidence points to an artificial context or a grouping of either sayings or narrative units. I will occasionally refer to the gospel of John to help clarify the life setting in the ministry of Jesus, especially the crucifixion, burial, and resurrection of

Jesus. This book was not written to be read by itself, but as a supplement to the primary texts--the canonical gospels. I recommend that the reader also obtain a gospel parallel such as Gospel Parallels, (Thomas Nelson Publishers: Nashville, 1992) edited by Bruce Throckmorton or Synopsis of the Four Gospels, (United Bible Societies, 1982) edited by Kurt Aland.

In recent years there has been a large amount of material published on Jesus--some scholarly, some of it aimed toward the clergy, some of it merely interested in the historical Jesus. All of these approaches have merit. However, I chose to write a different kind of book about Jesus. I wrote this book for the general reader or non-specialist. Moreover, I intend not only to educate the reader on the life of Jesus, but also to build faith in him as the Son of God.

I have endeavored to avoid technical terminology in favor of more accessible language for the general student. At certain places, I have briefly summarized the critical issues behind a particular passage, but these are always done in a user-friendly manner. I have tried to be honest with the gospel text and avoid simplistic explanations for difficult questions. This book would not have been written if it had not been for the guidance and editorial skills of Laura Morgan, Noreen Bryant, and Debbie Haskell. Their contributions have made it possible for me to produce this book. They have my profound gratitude.

My final thanks goes to two men who are now with the Lord, my professors Frank Pack and Ray Summers. Dr. Pack, my advisor and mentor at Pepperdine University, first invited me to teach a life of Christ course. Dr. Summers of Baylor University opened to me the world of scholarship in the synoptic gospels—a world that is ever-changing but always fascinating to me. I will always consider myself their student.

Rochester Hills, Michigan January 2006

Chapter 1

The Life of Jesus and Historical Research

For the first 1700 years of Christian history, most people accepted the historical accuracy of the four gospels and believed that Jesus of Nazareth lived, was baptized by John in the Jordan, carried out a three-year ministry in ancient Palestine, performed miracles, was crucified and later raised from the dead. However, in the 18th century, there arose among some intellectuals serious doubt concerning the historical Jesus. At that time there was a philosophical movement sweeping Europe known as the Enlightenment. Many Enlightenment philosophers and religious thinkers believed that human reason alone was the key to understanding truth. It was generally believed that empirical and/or scientific evidence was needed in order to learn any truth. Many thought that the New Testament gospels were simply collections of myths and legends with little historical accuracy. Some of the scholars believed that only a small core of the historical Jesus had been preserved in the gospels. Others even suggested that Jesus never existed, that he was simply a creation by a religious cult.

These ideas helped start a scholarly movement known later as "the quest for the historical Jesus." These scholars believed that it was possible to recover the real historical Jesus through scientific and historical study. The working assumption was that underneath several layers of tradition and myth lay that kernel of the original Jesus of history. The initial result of this movement was that the historical Jesus embedded in the gospel story was simply a human being, a Jew. This Jesus was a religious and ethical teacher. He performed no miracles. His teachings simply stressed that God is the heavenly father, that all people are children of God, and that to be a Christian required that one show love and compassion toward his or her fellow human beings. There was no doctrine of the church, nor of heaven.

During the first half of the 20th century, a variety of sophisticated methods to study the gospels were developed. Many scholars who had been influenced by 20th century theological perspectives adopted these methods. The result was an increasing skepticism concerning the historical value of the gospels. Some scholars claimed that the gospel message would speak with more power and meaning if it was set free from the mythological worldview of ancient society. However, when that myth has been removed, virtually nothing is left of the historical Jesus. Thus, according to this view, the New Testament portrayal of a supernatural Jesus was a product of later Christian imagination. In the early 1950's, there arose a movement among gospel scholars to reaffirm more historical accuracy in the New Testament gospels' portrayal of Jesus. While there continues to be a small group of scholars who hold to skeptical views similar to those who were part of the original "Quest," there has been a growing acceptance of the gospels as a reliable testimony to Jesus of Nazareth.

The primary evidence for Jesus of Nazareth are the four gospels of the New Testament. Outside of the New Testament sources, the material is rather sparse. However, there are a few interesting statements concerning Jesus by people who were not Christians themselves. The evidence which comes from Jewish sources is mostly hostile to Christianity, but, nonetheless, still confirms much of what the gospels say about Jesus.

Evidence for the Historical Jesus From Ancient Jewish Sources

Josephus (AD 37-100)

Josephus was a Jewish historian who wrote essentially to portray the Jewish people in a positive light to the Roman authorities. In his *Antiquities of the Jews*, there is recorded a remarkable passage about Jesus:

> (3) Now there was about this time Jesus, a wise man, if it be lawful to call him a man; for he was a doer of wonderful works, a teacher of such men as receive the truth with pleasure. He drew over to him both many of the Jews and many of the Gentiles. He was [the] Christ. And when Pilate, at the suggestion of the principal men amongst us, had condemned him to the cross, those that loved him at the first did not forsake him; for he appeared to them alive again the third day; as the divine prophets had foretold these and ten thousand other wonderful things concerning him. And the tribe of Christians, so named from him, are not extinct at this day. (Book 18.3.3)

In its current state it is widely believed that this passage was reworked by an unknown Christian. There is no evidence from other sources that Josephus ever considered Jesus to be the Messiah. However, it is possible that part of this statement is authentic. The text claims that Jesus was a wise man, that he performed miracles, and was a teacher. Josephus also knows that Jesus was crucified by order of Pilate. Moreover, following the death of Jesus, a community of believers was formed. Most likely, the references to Jesus' divinity and resurrection were indications of Christian additions, though it does reflect a very early opinion of Jesus by his followers. A second passage in Josephus may be more important:

> Festus was now dead, and Albinus was but upon the road; so he assembled the sanhedrin of judges, and brought before them the brother of Jesus, who was called Christ, whose name was James, and some others, [or, some of his companions]; and when he had formed an accusation against them as breakers of the law, he delivered them to be stoned. (20:9:1)

This is a narrative of the death of James the brother of Jesus, called the Christ. Nowhere in the passage does Josephus refer to Jesus as the Messiah. In fact, he appears to reject this notion. Thus it is likely that this passage was written by Josephus. Consequently, this text shows that Josephus knew of Jesus and that some had considered him to be the Messiah.

Interpretations of the Rabbis of the first two centuries

Despite the vast amount of ancient Jewish literature available, relatively little is said of Jesus. When brought together, however, the testimony of rabbis who lived soon after Jesus often agrees with the gospel record. Here are two well-known quotations:

> It is tradition that Rabbi Eliezer said to the wise, "Did not Ben Stada [Jesus] bring spells from Egypt in a cut which was upon his flesh?" They said to him, "He was a fool." Rabbi Hisda said, "The husband was Stada, the paramour was Pandira [Jesus' supposed natural father]." The husband was Pappos ben Jehudah, the father was Stada. The mother was Miriam the dresser of women's hair. . . . Such a one has been false to her husband." (b Shabbath 104)

> It was taught: On the day before the Passover they hanged Jesus. A herald went before him for forty days [proclaiming], "He will be stoned, because he practiced magic and enticed Israel to go astray. Let anyone who knows anything in his favor come forward and plead for him." But nothing was found in his favor, and they hanged him on the day before the Passover. (b. Sanhedrin 43a)

The records claim that:

1. Jesus was an illegitimate son of an adulteress by a Roman soldier named Pandira or Panthera (possible corruption of the Greek for "Virgin").
2. Forty days before Jesus' execution, a preacher went about announcing what was about to happen.
3. Jesus was often referred to as one who practiced sorcery. Later rabbinical comments show that they affirmed that Jesus lived, that he was a religious teacher, that he was regarded as one who practiced healing, and that he was executed.

Celsus

Celsus was a pagan who lived during the 2nd century. Although Celsus' own work has not survived, the early Christian scholar Origen apparently quoted from Celsus' written attack on Christianity in order to respond to him. In one passage, Celsus presents a scandalous interpretation of Jesus' life, probably based on a Jewish revisionist version of the story of Jesus. However, despite the scandalous nature of this version, this narrative unwittingly acknowledges the historicity of much of the Christian tradition concerning Jesus:

> He portrays the Jew having a conversation with Jesus himself, refuting him on many charges. First, *he fabricated the story of his birth from a virgin;* and he reproaches him because *he came from a Jewish village and from a poor country woman who made her living by spinning.* He says that *she was driven out by her husband, who was a carpenter by trade, when she was convicted of adultery.* Then he says that *after she had been driven out by her husband and while she was wandering disgracefully, she secretly bore Jesus.* He says that *because (Jesus) was poor he hired himself out as a laborer in Egypt, and there learned certain magical powers which the Egyptians are proud to have. He returned full of pride in these powers, and gave himself the title of God.* (Against Celsus 1.28)

The Evidence for the Historical Jesus From Ancient Roman Historians

Pliny the Younger (AD 62-113) Letter to Trajan:

As the Roman governor of Bithynia, Pliny asked Emperor Trajan for guidance on how to deal with the Christians. The following quotation includes some interesting descriptions of early Christians as viewed from the eyes of an unbeliever.

Pliny to Trajan:

> They [Christians] . . . declared that the sum total of their guilt or error amounted to no more than this: they had met regularly before dawn on a fixed day to chant verses alternately amongst themselves in honor of Christ as if to a god and also to bind themselves by oath, not for any criminal purpose, but to abstain from theft, robbery, and adultery, to

> commit no breach of trust and not to deny a deposit when called upon to restore it. After this ceremony it had been their custom to disperse and reassemble later to take food of an ordinary harmless kind; but they had in fact given up this practice since my edict, issued on your instructions, which banned all political societies. This made me decide it was all the more necessary to extract the truth by torture from two slave-women, whom they call deaconesses. I found nothing but a degenerate sort of cult carried to extravagant lengths. (Letters, 10. 96-97).

From Pliny, we learn that the early Christians worshipped Jesus as divine, devoted themselves to moral living, and shared together a fellowship meal, possibly the Lord's Supper, on the first day of the week.

Suetonius (AD 75-110) Lives of the Twelve Caesars:

Suetonius was a contemporary of Pliny who recorded an incident in Rome, possibly involving Christians. This record does not enlighten historians on Jesus of Nazareth, except showing that the Christian movement was already in Rome by the middle of the first century during the reign of Claudius (A.D. 41-54). Suetonius refers to a disturbance among the Jews in Rome which led Emperor Claudius to expel them from Rome:

> He [Claudius] expelled the Jews from Rome, since they were always making disturb ances because of the instigator Chrestus (Claudius 25.4)

The name ***Chrestos or Chrestus*** is probably a corruption of ***Christos*** or Christ or the Christ movement or Christians. Possibly the disturbance arose from Jewish opposition to Christianity, i.e., they opposed and persecuted the Christian preachers. However, it may have been a disturbance caused by overly zealous and aggressive Christian evangelists.

Tacitus (AD 55-117) - The Annals of Imperial Rome

Tacitus, who is generally regarded as the greatest Roman historian, described the great fire of Rome in vivid detail during the reign of Nero (AD 54-68):

> But neither human effort nor the emperor's generosity nor the placating of the gods ended the scandalous belief that the fire had been ordered. Therefore, to put down the rumor, Nero substituted as culprits and punished in the most unusual ways those hated for their shameful acts, whom the crowd called "Chrestians" [other translations read "Christians"]. The founder of this name, Christ, had been executed in the reign of Tiberius by the procurator Pontius Pilate. Suppressed for a time, the deadly superstition erupted again not only in Judea, the origin of this evil, but also in the city [Rome], where all things horrible and shameful from everywhere come together and become popular. Therefore, first those who admitted to it were arrested, then on their information a very large multitude was convicted, not so much for the crime of arson as for hatred of the human race. Derision was added to their end: they were covered with the skins of wild animals and torn to death by dogs; or they were crucified and when the day ended they were burned as torches. Nero provided his gardens for the spectacle and gave a show in his circus, mixing with the people in charioteer's clothing, or standing on his racing chariot. Therefore, a feeling of pity arose despite a guilt which deserved the most exemplary punishment, because it was felt that they were being destroyed not for the public good but for the ferocity of one man. (Annals 15.44)

Tacitus records that Nero blamed the fire on the Christians to divert blame from himself. Despite Tacitus' antagonism of Christians, he indicates that there was a large Christian community in Rome. Moreover, this movement had been founded by Christ who had been condemned to death by Pontius Pilate during the reign of Tiberius.

The Evidence of the Historical Jesus From the New Testament

The vast majority of the information available concerning Jesus comes from the four gospels. However, the earliest witness concerning the historical Jesus is Paul, since his writings came before the written gospels. Drawing only upon the writings attributed to Paul, the following can be known about Jesus:

1. Jesus was a descendant of David - Romans 1:3.
2. Jesus lived under the Law of Moses: He was a Jew - Galatians 4:4.
3. Jesus had a brother named James - 1 Corinthians 9:5; Galatians 1:19.
4. Jesus established the Lord's Supper - 1 Corinthians 11:23-26.
5. Jesus was tried under Pilate - 1 Timothy 6:13.
6. Jesus was crucified, buried and raised from the dead on the third day. - 1 Corinthians 15:3-4.
7. Jesus, as risen, appeared to many different people. - 1 Corinthians 15:5-8.

Moreover, there appear to be allusions to and virtual quotations of Jesus in Paul's writings. While there is debate as to whether some passages are truly allusions to the sayings of Jesus, others are more likely to have originated from him. For example:

1. Paul refers to the command of the Lord (Jesus) concerning divorce. - 1 Corinthians 7:10 (Mark 10:2-9).
2. Paul states that "the Lord has commanded that those who preach the gospel should receive their living from the gospel." - 1 Corinthians 9:14 (Luke 10:1-7)
3. Paul cites Jesus' institution of the Lord's Supper. - 1 Corinthians 11:23-25 (Matthew 26:26-29; Mark 14:22-25; Luke 22:14-20).
4. Paul describes the second coming of Jesus to be like "a thief in the night." - 1 Thessalonians 5:1-7 (Luke 21:34-36).
5. Paul exhorts Christians to "bless those who persecute you." - Romans 12:14 (Matthew 5:44)
6. Paul declares that "love is the fulfillment of the law." and that "The entire law is summed up in a single command: "Love your neighbor as yourself." - Romans 13:8-10; Galatians 5:14 (Mark 12:31 and Matthew 22:39)
7. Paul says that Christians have the assurance to address God as "Abba Father." - Romans 8:15; Galatians 4:6 (Mark 14:36)

While less extensive, the rest of the New Testament further supports the gospel's portrayal of Jesus. Nearly all of them make some reference to the death and resurrection of Jesus. In addition to these, there are several other passages which mention something about Jesus' life and teachings. The following is a partial list:

The Acts of the Apostles

1. Judas betrayed Jesus and later suffered a horrible death. (1:16-18)
2. Jesus performed many miracles (signs, wonders, and works of power). (2:22)
3. Herod, Pilate, and the people of Israel participated in the death of Jesus. (4:27)
4. Jesus' ministry began after the ministry of John the Baptist. He was anointed with the Holy Spirit. The ministry of Jesus, during which he performed many miracles, began in Galilee. Afterwards Jesus moved to Judea, specifically Jerusalem, where the authorities put him to death by "hanging him on a tree." Yet God raised him up and he appeared to his disciples, whom he commissioned to testify that forgiveness of sins is available through the name of Jesus. (10:34-43)
5. John the Baptist preached a baptism of repentance. John the Baptist did not consider himself worthy of even untying the sandals of Jesus. The Jews asked Pilate to have Jesus killed. After his death, Jesus was buried in a tomb. Afterwards, Jesus was raised from the dead and appeared to those who had been with him in Galilee and Jerusalem. (13:23-31)
6. Paul refers to "the words of the Lord Jesus" and "It is more blessed to give than to receive." (20:35)

Hebrews

1. Jesus was tempted to sin. (2:18; 4:15)

2. In deep anguish, Jesus prayed that God might spare his life. (5:7)
3. Jesus suffered and died outside the city gates of Jerusalem (13:2)

James (Allusions to the Sermon on the Mount)

1. One cannot be a friend of both the world and God (4:4; Matthew 6:24)
2. "Your riches have rotted, and your clothes are moth-eaten. Your gold and silver have rusted, and their rust will be evidence against you." (5:2-3; Matthew 5:19-20)
3. "let your 'Yes' be yes and your 'No' be no. . . ." (5:12; Matthew 5:34-37)

2 Peter (The Transfiguration of Jesus)

1. "But we had been eyewitnesses of his majesty. For he received honor and glory from God the Father when that voice was conveyed to him by the Majestic Glory, saying, 'This is my son, my Beloved, with whom I am well pleased.' We ourselves heard this voice come from heaven, while we were with him on the holy mountain." (2 Peter 1:16b-18)

1 and 2 John

1. Christians are to practice the New Commandment, which means to love one another. (1John 2:7-12; 2 John 5)

The Evidence of the Historical Jesus From Outside the New Testament: The Gospel of Thomas

After the formation of the New Testament, early Christians continued to write about Jesus and Christian faith. The vast majority of the references to Jesus came directly from the four canonical gospels. A smaller portion of material was either created by some Christian writer or legends which arose concerning Jesus, such as those concerning his childhood. However, there is other ancient material, which some scholars believe to contain authentic information about or sayings by Jesus. The most important of these is a second-century work known as the Gospel of Thomas. While the work had been cited by other early Christians, it wasn't until 1945 that this work was discovered among the Nag Hammadi documents--a collection of religious writings by an early sect of Christians. The Gospel of Thomas is a collection of 114 sayings attributed to Jesus. Many of the sayings are very similar to sayings found in the Synoptic gospels, but others are unique. The significance of the Gospel of Thomas is twofold. First, it is possible that the Gospel of Thomas contains authentic sayings not found anywhere else. Here are five sayings which have been suggested as possibly authentic sayings of Jesus:

> . . . you do not know who I am, but have become as the Jews. They love the tree, they hate its fruit; they love the fruit, they hate the tree. (Logion 43)
>
> Jesus said, "A man cannot mount two horses; he cannot stretch two bows. (Logion 47a)
>
> Jesus said, "He who is near me is near the fire, and he who is far from me is far from the Kingdom." (Logion 82)
>
> Jesus said, "The Kingdom of the [Father] is like a woman who was carrying a jar which was full of meal. While she was walking on a distant road, the handle of the jar broke; the meal spilled out behind her onto the road. She did not know; she was not aware of the accident. After she came to her house, she put the jar down and found it empty." (Logion 97)
>
> Jesus said, "Woe to the Pharisees; they are like a dog lying in the oxen's food trough, for he does not eat nor let the oxen eat." (Logion 102)

Second, some scholars believe that the sayings in the Gospel of Thomas, which are similar to those in the Synoptics, did not come from the

Synoptics, but from an earlier independent source. However, there is not full agreement on this latter theory. Many other scholars believe that Matthew, Mark and Luke still should be regarded as the primary if not sole source for the sayings of Jesus in the Gospel of Thomas. Nevertheless, all scholars recognize that the Gospel of Thomas is a valuable testimony to the significance of the sayings of Jesus for the early church.

Conclusion: Jesus-Fact or Fiction?

Throughout the past two thousand years, the biblical testimony concerning Jesus of Nazareth has been critically analyzed by believer and skeptic alike. Despite all the criticism and doubts that have been raised, faith in Jesus has persisted and even flourished. For more than two centuries, creative theories have been presented that raised doubts about whether Jesus was nothing more than an elaborate mythical figure. Indeed there are still people whose theories continue to challenge the traditional view of Jesus. Nevertheless, there are also many others whose articulate and scholarly defense of the historical reliability of the gospel record has help lend credence to the belief in Jesus as the Son of God. The historical information surveyed in this chapter shows that the claims of Matthew, Mark, Luke, and John were not entirely unknown by the ancient world. Whatever the ancients who knew of the Christian movement thought of Jesus, they most likely thought that he at least was a real person--a Jew who lived in Palestine in the first century, that he was a religious teacher who was eventually executed by the Roman authorities. Obviously for the Christian, there is much more to faith in Jesus than a belief that Jesus was a historical person. That Jesus died on a cross is an event in history, which even the skeptic can acknowledge. However, for one to claim that Jesus' death was for the sins of humankind--that men and women may be brought back into fellowship with God through the blood of Jesus--is to make a statement of faith, which the historian cannot prove or disprove. This book was written with the assumption that as we investigate the story of Jesus in the gospels we may do so with confidence that the story is about faith that is firmly rooted in history.

Chapter 2

Introduction to the Synoptic Gospels

What Does "New Testament" Mean?

This study will examine the testimony of Jesus primarily found in the gospels according to Matthew, Mark and Luke. But before embarking on this study, it is important that some basic information about the New Testament and the gospels first be understood. The expression "New Testament" should more accurately be translated "New Covenant." The term "covenant" refers to an agreement or contract concerning a relationship between two parties. The concept of covenant originated in the ancient middle eastern practice of "suzerainty covenants," in which the party in the position of strength offers the terms for relationship with a weaker party. For example, a conquering king might offer terms for a peaceful relationship with a certain village or city. The king may promise to ensure the city's safety from invasion, the opportunity to carry out business, and prosper from profits gained from her enterprises. But the city must agree to recognize this person as the true king, be loyal to him, obey his laws, and pay prescribed taxes to him. Any disobedience or attempt to align with an opposing power will render the covenant null and void, thus leaving the village vulnerable for the king to attack and plunder her. On the other hand, if the king fails to live up to his part of the contract, the village is legally free from the obligations of the covenant. So, in a sense, both parties must obligate themselves to the terms of the covenant.

The covenant that God established at Mount Sinai with Israel had some of these characteristics. In the Old Testament, both Israel and God promised to be faithful to the terms of the covenant. Israel's covenant relationship with God was based on obedience to the Law and trust in God. Of particular importance were the commandments concerning sacrifices, worship regulations, dietary restrictions, and moral law. Conversely, God promised to bless, protect, and guide Israel. Ironically, recorded history shows that Israel repeatedly violated the covenant, but that God continued to be faithful.

The claim of the earliest Christians was that a new covenant had been established by Jesus, in fulfillment of prophecy. Jesus claimed that his death and resurrection would usher in the new covenant based on the love and mercy of God. As a result of the work of Jesus, the new covenant would be received as a gift of grace, and believers could receive the blessings of divine favor.

What Does "Gospel" Mean?

It is generally known that "gospel" means "good news." The term "gospel" was often used in the secular world to refer to the announcement of some happy event. The Old Testament prophet Isaiah used the Hebrew counterpart to refer to the proclamation, a message of deliverance for Israel from exile (See Isaiah 40:1-11; 52:1-10; 61:1-11). Jesus quoted from Isaiah 61 in his sermon at Nazareth,, and then stated that this prophecy was fulfilled in their hearing (Luke 4:16-21). Apparently, Jesus chose to adopt Isaiah's use of "good news" as a message of salvation.

The gospel of which Jesus spoke was a message concerning the coming of the kingdom of God. He declared that God's promises had been fulfilled and that one must repent and believe the message in order to be ready to enter the kingdom (Mark 1:14-15). Later, the apostles preached that God had fulfilled his promises through Jesus, especially through his death and resurrection. Therefore, the Gospel was the message of God's salvation for all. Later the term "gospel" came to mean the story of Jesus in written form. This may be because the early preaching of the apostles may have retold the story of Jesus (See Peter's sermon to Cornelius in Acts 10:34-43).

Yet the written gospels are not pure history or biography. Only about 60 days of Jesus' life is recorded in all four gospels. A comparison of the four gospels reveal they do not always agree with each other in the chronology of events or the exact wording of Jesus' sayings. Each gospel was written to communicate the "Gospel" message to the readers. Thus the gospels contained more a message of salvation and an invitation to faith. These gospels may have also been written to apply the teachings of Jesus to issues and problems facing the early church.

The Growth of the Gospel Tradition

Most scholars believe that the written gospels came about through a process of development from strict oral tradition to the final written documents. The following is a summary of the most commonly accepted theory concerning that development. Essentially, that development took place in three general stages:

1. The Oral Stage (AD 30-50)
2. The First Written Stage (AD 50-70)
3. The Final Written Stage (AD 65-100)

The Oral Stage (AD 30 – 50)

During the Oral Stage, it is believed that some of the early Christians memorized the sayings of Jesus and shared these with the Church. It was also likely that there were many eyewitnesses to the works of Jesus who remembered what he did and retold those stories to others. Most scholars believe that the oral tradition was preserved in certain identifiable forms which were preserved in the written gospel. Some of these forms are the following:

1. **The Passion Story**. The story of the last week and hours of Jesus' life. This story may have been preserved in a particular form in order to explain how it was possible that the innocent Son of God could have been tried, convicted, condemned, and executed.

2. **Pronouncement Stories**. These are brief narratives in which there is dialogue between Jesus and some other group (usually the religious leaders). The purpose of these type of stories is to highlight a very specific and memorable saying of Jesus, such as: "render to Caesar the things that are Caesar's and to God the things that are God's."
3. **Miracle Stories.** These are stories which demonstrate the power of God in Jesus during his ministry. Usually these stories are told in a particular style: a need is brought to Jesus' attention; a description of the problem is given; Jesus usually says and perhaps also does something; a description of the new condition is presented.
4. **Sayings of Jesus.** These are sayings of Jesus in which there does not appear to be a close connection between the saying and the literary context in which the saying is placed. Some scholars believe that at least Matthew collected many of these sayings and grouped them into large blocks of teachings for purposes of presenting the teachings of Jesus all in one place.
5. **Parables.** The parables are one of the unique aspects of Jesus' work as a teacher. While Jesus did not invent the parable form, most scholars agree that he developed the parable to a level of sophistication far beyond what anyone else had already done. Most parables have a very identifiable structure or style to them.
6. **Stories about Jesus.** These are the stories in the gospels in which the uniqueness and divine nature of Jesus is emphasized through these narratives. These stories include the birth, baptism, and temptation of Jesus. Also one may examine the confession of Peter at Caesarea Philippi and the transfiguration.

First Written Stage (AD 50 – 70)

Many scholars believe that before the gospels were finally written some early Christians first wrote down some stories or sayings which were later found in the written gospel, such as a collection of parables, a collection of similar miracle stories, or a particular memorable event or saying. Some evidence exists that the early church compiled several passages from the Old Testament which were believed to have significance for Christianity.

Usually, the passages were seen as prophecies of Jesus or the Christian age. Matthew in particular may have drawn from such a source since he cites so many important Old Testament passages.

The Final Written Stage (AD 65 – 100)

This is the period when the gospels were written as they are preserved in the Bible. While there are a variety of opinions concerning the date, place of writing, and authorship of the gospels as they appear in the Bible, the majority of scholars believe that Mark was the first gospel to be written. Based on information from early church tradition and possible evidence from the gospel itself, most scholars believe that **Mark** was written somewhere between **A.D. 65-70**. Matthew appears to have been composed in Syria, possibly Antioch. While some are convinced that **Matthew** was also written around A.D. 65, others, including this author, believe the first canonical gospel was written later, perhaps between **A.D. 80-90**. The date and setting for **Luke** has been more difficult for scholars to determine. As with Matthew, an early and late date theory is also possible for Luke. There are some who believe Luke was written in the early **'60s**, while others, again including this author, opt for a date in the **'80s**. Nearly all scholars agree that the gospel of **John** was the last of the four gospels to be written, probably between **A.D.95-100** and from Roman Asia, known today as Turkey. A close reading of each of the gospels will show that none of them clearly identify the author. By the end of the second century, however, it was unanimously believed that the names Matthew, Mark, Luke, and John were the names of the actual authors, two who were apostles (Matthew and John) and two missionary companions of Paul and Peter (Mark and Luke[Paul only]). Thus, most likely the superscriptions: "The Gospel According to Matthew," "The Gospel According to Mark," "The Gospel According to Luke," and "The Gospel According to John" were created by the early church and affixed to the beginning of the appropriate gospel. Nevertheless, while the gospels may have been pseudonymous, the early Christians believed they knew who were authors of these works and their convictions should at least be respected.

Very early the four gospels were gathered together in an authoritative testimony concerning Jesus' life. In later centuries other writings also known as gospels appeared, but they were never widely accepted by the Church.

The Synoptic Gospels

The first three gospels are commonly known as the "Synoptic Gospels." The term *synoptic* comes from two words which together means "to see together." This means that Matthew, Mark and Luke are very similar in their narratives of Jesus, while John is quite different. In order to appreciate the remarkable similarities between the synoptic gospels, note the following statistics:

- Almost ½ of Matthew is in Mark
- Over 1/3 of Luke is in Mark
- Over 95% of Mark is in either or both Matthew and Luke
- Luke and Matthew have a significant amount of material in common which is not in Mark.
- Matthew and Luke have a considerable amount of material which is unique to the individual gospels.

Several solutions have been proposed to explain both the similarities and the differences that exist with the synoptic gospels. The following are the most popular explanations:

1. **Oral Tradition**. All the gospels arose independently but all were drawn from a common tradition.
2. **Mutual Interdependence**. This theory proposes that one gospel was written first, a second borrowed from the first, and the third borrowed from both the first and second. For example: Matthew>Mark>Luke.
3. **Two-Source Theory**. Essentially two sources were responsible for the writing of the synoptic gospels. The most common version of this suggests that Mark and a sayings of Jesus source (called "Q," from the German word *quelle*, meaning source), perhaps written about AD 50-65, were the two primary sources for Matthew and

Luke. Matthew and Luke may have also had access to other sources, some written and others oral.

4. **Four-Source Theory**. This is an expansion of the two-source theory. This theory states that there were four sources between the Synoptic Gospels: Mark , a sayings source (Q), Matthew's unique material (M), and Luke's special material (L). One theory proposes that Mark was probably written about 65 in Rome. Also some have suggested that Q may have been written about 50 from Antioch of Syria. Matthew's special source (M) is thought to have been written from Jerusalem about 60. This source has particular concern with the fulfillment of Old Testament prophecy and Jesus' relationship to Judaism. And lastly, L (Luke's special source) may have been written about 60, possibly from Caesarea. This source probably stressed God's mercy and Jesus' concern for the outcast.

Conclusion Concerning the Growth of the Gospel Tradition

While there is rarely full agreement among the scholars concerning the human origins of the gospels, some general consensus has emerged, which this study of the life of Jesus has assumed. First, most likely the early church preserved both the sayings of and stories about Jesus, first in oral and later in written form. Second, Mark was most likely the first gospel to be written, dated about AD 65 from Rome. Third, Matthew and Luke most likely had access to and utilized Mark and a common source, consisting of sayings of Jesus, which has been labeled Q. In addition to the above items, scholars also widely agreed that the gospel according to Matthew was written between AD 70 and 85, possibly from Antioch of Syria, and Luke was likewise written between AD 70-85, possibly from Philippi or some other Pauline missionary post.

Whatever the exact truth concerning the origins of the written gospels, the testimony of the gospels concerning the life and ministry of Jesus of Nazareth can be trusted as historically reliable. In the pages of these written testimonies, the reader encounters the man whom millions have confessed to be the Son of God. That is also my confession.

An Overview of Jesus' Life According to the Synoptic Gospels

1. The Early Years
   - A. The birth of Jesus
     - Approximate date: 4 BC
     - Place: Bethlehem
     - Gospel sources: Matthew and Luke
   - B. Jesus at 12 in the temple at Jerusalem: Luke 2
   - C. Jesus' baptism and temptation
     - Approximate date: AD 27
     - Jesus' baptism marks God's acceptance of Jesus as His son
     - Jesus' temptation was the first occasion when he was challenged concerning his attitude toward the nature of his ministry and miraculous power
     - Gospel sources: Matthew, Mark, and Luke
2. Early Galilean Ministry
   - A. Area of Ministry: Mostly Galilee
   - B. Key Events
     - The announcement at Nazareth
     - Miracles of healing
     - Choosing the twelve disciples
     - Jesus answered the critics concerning his attitude toward the Law of Moses
     - The Sermon on the Mount
     - The limited commission of the twelve disciples
     - The death of John the Baptist
     - The Feeding of the 5000
3. Latter Galilean Ministry
   - A. Waning popularity - Many people stopped following Jesus when they saw he was not going to be a military messiah or leader.
   - B. Jesus toured the northern provinces when the atmosphere in Galilee was not safe.
     - Peter confessed faith in Jesus as the Messiah at Caesarea Philippi

- Jesus was transfigured on a mountain before three of his disciples

C. Hostility toward Jesus from Jewish leaders was increasing and becoming more public. The leaders apparently considered him to be a threat.
- Jesus had rejected their traditions on the law, especially the sabbath
- Jesus had condemned their hypocrisy, legalism, and bigotry
- Jesus was becoming more open concerning his claim to be the Messiah

D. Jesus spent more time instructing the disciples on humility, self-sacrifice, and love

E. The Perean Ministry (Found only in Luke)
- Perea refers to the territory east of the Jordan river
- This section contains many of the more well known parables of Jesus: The Good Samaritan, The Prodigal Son, The Rich Man, Lazarus and others

F. Jesus' journey to Jerusalem
- Jesus taught concerning marriage, divorce and children
- Jesus told the rich young ruler to sell all he had and give it to the poor
- Jesus accepted Zacchaeus
- Jesus anointed by Mary with costly perfume

4. The Final Week in Jerusalem

A. Sunday: The triumphant entry of Jesus into Jerusalem

B. Monday: Jesus cursed the fig tree and cleansed the temple *Matthew, Mark, and Luke record that Jesus cleansed the temple in the last week of his earthly ministry, while John records a cleansing very early in his gospel. It is unlikely that Jesus cleansed the temple twice, since such an act done once would have been viewed with extreme seriousness by the leaders. So it is generally agreed that John chose to place the story early in his story for a specific literary purpose. Matthew, Mark, and Luke are generally regarded as preserving the original time of the event.*

C. Tuesday: Day of teaching, parables, questions, woes, and prophecy
D. Wednesday: Judas agrees to betray Jesus
E. Thursday: Passover
  - Institution of the Lord's Supper
  - Jesus prayed in the garden of Gethsemane
  - Jesus was betrayed by Judas
  - The night trials or hearings

F. Friday: Formal condemnation of Jesus by the Sanhedrin
  - Trials before Pilate and Herod
  - Condemnation of Jesus by Pilate
  - Crucifixion
  - Burial of Jesus

G. Saturday: Jesus in the tomb
H. Sunday: The resurrection of Jesus

Chapter 3

The Birth of Jesus

Introduction

The gospels of Matthew and Luke present two different accounts of the birth of Jesus. Matthew opens his gospel as a genealogy of Jesus, beginning with Abraham and ending with Jesus. The genealogical record was designed to show that not only was Jesus truly a descendant of Abraham, a Jew, but that he was also the son of David, of royal blood. As son of David, Jesus is qualified to be king, and thus the messiah of Israel. On the other hand, Luke begins by narrating the birth of the one who would prepare the way for Jesus, John the Baptist.

Preparation for the Birth of Jesus according to Luke

The Annunciation of John (Luke 1:5-10)

Luke tells the reader that John's father was a certain priest named Zechariah. He also notes that his mother, Elizabeth, was a daughter of Aaron, making her also from a priestly family. Like Sarah and Abraham of old, this old couple was hopelessly childless. Undoubtedly, Luke expects the reader to see the similarity between this elderly childless couple and those mentioned in the Old Testament. As with the birth of Isaac to Sarah and Abraham, so also the birth of John to Elizabeth and Zechariah, will be the result of the direct and miraculous intervention of God.

Little is known about the various priestly divisions that existed in those days. What does seem to be clear is that, due to the large number of priests, each had the privilege to serve in the temple only once in a lifetime. The text indicates that it was Zechariah's turn to have the responsibility of offering incense to the Lord. The incense was offered on the Altar of Incense in the Holy Place of the Temple. Apparently the incense which Zechariah offered to God served as a symbol of the prayers of God's people. Most likely this offering was done before the morning sacrifice.

The message of the angel Gabriel (Luke 1:11-23)

The angel announced that Zechariah's prayer had been heard by God, and as a result he would have a son and that his name would be John. Though Elizabeth was barren, God would make it possible for her to become pregnant and give birth to their son. This recalls the Old Testament stories of the births of Isaac to Abraham and Sarah (Genesis 12-21), Jacob to Isaac and Rebecca (Genesis 25:21-25), Samuel to Elkanah and Hannah (1 Samuel 1:9-20), and Samson to Manoah and his unnamed wife (Judges 13:2-24).

It is generally believed that the statement that John would not drink wine or strong drink suggests that he would be a Nazirite (Numbers 6). A Nazarite was one who took a vow before God and others to be devoted to God in a special way. He was not to drink or eat anything made from grapes, nor was he to cut his hair nor touch anything that was designated by cultic law to be ritually unclean. Some took the vow for a specific and limited period of time. Others were devoted to this vow for life. Like Samson, John was to be a lifetime Nazirite. The angel also promised that this child would be filled with the Holy Spirit. Such a designation was usually reserved for a prophet (see Micah 3:8 for comparison). Perhaps the significance of this was that it was generally believed that the voice of the prophet had ended with Malachi or the last Old Testament prophet. If John really was a prophet, then it would mean that God was once again speaking to His people. John's message would be a call for people to change their ways, to repent. His ministry would be to prepare the people for the coming of the messiah.

Like Abraham of old, when Zechariah heard he was to have a son, he expressed doubt. After all, both he and his wife were old and physically unable to have children, so the old priest wanted some assurance that this was really going to take place. The angel Gabriel assured him that this promise was truly from God, but because of his lack of belief, he would be unable to speak until the child was born. When he came out of the temple, Zechariah was unable to give the benediction, which led the people to conclude that he had a vision.

The Annunciation to Mary (Luke 1:26-38)

The text indicates that six months after the annunciation of the future birth of John the angel appeared to Mary. While later church tradition is full of legendary stories about Mary and her parents, very little is actually known about Mary. Luke describes her as a virgin who lived in Nazareth of Galilee. Moreover, since Mary is a relative of Elizabeth, she is most likely from the priestly family.

Our biblical text states that Mary was "pledged to a man named Joseph." Such an arrangement was commonly known as a betrothal. A betrothal was something like a marriage engagement, but more binding. It was more like an incomplete marriage, often arranged by the parents. While a modern engagement can be nullified by either party at any time and for any reason, a betrothal could only be terminated by a divorce. Moreover, one was expected to be as faithful to his/her betrothed as to his/her spouse. While the modern marriage engagement is a type of public announcement of two people's intention to be married, a betrothal was more like a legal transaction between the two families. Usually there was a payment of an agreed-upon amount of money from one father to the other. Sometimes two families would agree on a betrothal while the future husband and wife were still small children.

The angel Gabriel told Mary that she was to become pregnant and give birth to a son, whose name would be Jesus. The name "Jesus" is the Greek form of the Hebrew Jeshua, or Joshua, and it means "The Lord is

Salvation." Mary also heard that God would give this child the throne of David, where he would reign over the House of Jacob (i.e., Israel) forever. Gabriel's message to Mary reveals that Jesus would truly be the anointed of the Lord, which is another way of saying "Messiah." As Son of God, Jesus is not only king, but also divine. Mary's question, "How can this be, since I am a virgin?" is similar to Zechariah's question (1:18). Apparently, though, he asked in doubt, while Mary asked out of confusion and fear. The angel answered that the Holy Spirit would miraculously cause her to become pregnant while still a virgin.

Special Topic: Objections to the Virgin Birth

Some scholars who do not believe the virgin birth of Jesus have argued that the New Testament writers borrowed from ancient myths of the births of a hero or half-man—half-god person such as Hercules, who was born as the result of Zeus having sex with a mortal woman. However, such an explanation is unconvincing for several reasons. First, no self-respecting Jew would have tolerated any view of God that would conceive of Him coming to earth to seduce women. In fact, the Jewish book of Enoch, written between 200-100 BC, interpreted the story in Genesis 6:1-4 to be about angels coming to earth to seduce mortal women and were later punished by God for this abomination. Secondly, the pregnancy is described as a completely asexual event. Rather, Mary was the recipient of a miracle. Thirdly, Jesus was a real historical person. Hercules and other like him were simply mythological beings. The fact that Mary became pregnant by miracle meant that Jesus was truly a unique person. For that reason, the angel said that the child would be holy, which means "different, separate, and set apart for God's purposes."

Mary visits Elizabeth - Luke 1:39-56

Luke narrates that Mary hurriedly went to visit her relative Elizabeth, since she too was expecting a child. In anticipation of events and testimony to take place in the future, the unborn John leaps in Elizabeth's womb, presumably in joyful response to the presence of the unborn Son of God.

Elizabeth also blesses Mary as if she knows that Mary's child will be even greater than hers. Then Luke records a song that Mary sang to God. This song has come to be known as "The Magnificat," and was sung by the early Christians in their assemblies. Mary's song is reminiscent of some Old Testament songs, especially that of Hannah in I Samuel 2:1-10. The song is a song of praise and thanksgiving to God for his care for the lowly. The song stresses on God's mercy and compassion to the poor, the weak, and the marginalized.

The Birth of John - Luke 1:57-80

When a son was born to Elizabeth and Zechariah, the primary topic of discussion was the naming of the child. Friends assumed the boy would be named after his father Zechariah, in accordance with tradition. However, Elizabeth contended that he would be called John as the angel directed. As the leader of the household, Zechariah wrote: "His name is John." While Zechariah may have simply been naming the child, it is also possible that he was declaring that God had already named the boy John, since he was to be specially devoted to the Lord. After that, Zechariah regained his ability to speak, and uttered the song now known as the "Benedictus." This song portrays John as the one who would prepare the way of the Lord. The song also speaks of the Messiah as the one God would raise up from the house of David to deliver God's people from their enemies, particularly Rome. Therefore, Zechariah understood John's mission: to prepare God's people for the one who would drive out the Romans from their lands and possibly reestablish the kingdom of Israel. Verse 80 is a summary statement of the maturing of John to adulthood. Luke says that he lived in the wilderness until he was called to begin his prophetic ministry. Some have contended that he lived with a desert monastic community known as the Essenes, but there is no hard evidence that this was true.

Preparation for the Birth of Jesus according to Matthew

Prevention of divorce - Matthew 1:18-25

While Luke records an angelic announcement to Mary, Matthew narrates an event in which Joseph learned the meaning and significance of Mary's pregnancy. When Joseph discovered that Mary was pregnant, he naturally assumed that she had been unfaithful to him. The Law of Moses prescribes the death penalty for adulterers, but it is doubtful that such was ever carried out with much frequency. Matthew does not mention the possibly of death; instead, he cites the public disgrace resulting from divorce. Consequently, Joseph decides to divorce her privately; and in so doing, Matthew describes him as a righteous man.

However, since Matthew has already stated that Mary was pregnant by the Holy Spirit, we know that Joseph is mistaken about Mary. Joseph is soon corrected, when he is instructed by an angel in a dream not to divorce her. From the angel, Joseph discovers the true cause of Mary's pregnancy (the Holy Spirit), and that this future son, Jesus, will save his people from their sins. Since the name "Jesus" means "the Lord is my Salvation," the angel is actually predicting that Jesus will live up to the meaning of his name.

Special Topic: Matthew's use of Isaiah 7:14

Matthew then quotes from Isaiah 7:14 concerning the prophecy about the birth of Jesus. However, the original context of Isaiah 7:14 suggests that the prophet was prophesying concerning someone who was to be born during Isaiah's lifetime. The southern kingdom of Judah had been threatened by the joint forces of the northern kingdom of Israel and the Syrians in order to force the Judean king to join their military alliance against the mighty Assyrian Empire. However, King Ahaz refused and thus faced the prospects of military attack. The prophet Isaiah encouraged Ahaz to ask the Lord for a sign, but he would not. Nevertheless, Isaiah provided a sign concerning a child born to a young woman. This child, perhaps King Hezekiah, would be both the sign and the means by which the enemies of Judah would be defeated. The Hebrew word, translated "virgin" in the Greek of the New

Testament, simply meant a young woman of marriageable age. Matthew, who cites Old Testament passages from the Greek translation of the Old Testament, known as the Septuagint, quotes Isaiah 7:14, in which the "young woman" is translated in Greek as "virgin." For Matthew, Isaiah 7:14 is a prophecy with a double fulfillment: one in the time of Old Testament Israel, and the other with the birth of Christ.

Special Topic: The date of the birth of Jesus

While the Bible does not indicate exactly when Jesus was born, the Nativity is placed within a particular period of time. One can determine the span of years of this period of time by examining the time references found in the text:

- Luke 1:1. Jesus was born when Herod was king in Judea (47 BC to 4 BC).
- Luke 2:1. Jesus was born during the reign of Emperor Augustus (27 BC to AD 14).
- Luke 3:1. The ministry of John the Baptist began in the 15th year of Tiberius (AD 11-14 to 37). Tiberius may have co-ruled from AD11-14. Thus the 15th year of Tiberius would have been from AD 26-29. According to Luke 3:23, Jesus was about 30 when he began his work. If Jesus' ministry coincided with the beginning of John's ministry (AD 26-29), then his birth would have taken place from about 4 BC to 1 BC. Note our current calendar is inaccurate by about 4 years. That is why historians suggest that Jesus may have born in 4 BC.
- Matthew 2:1-12. Jesus was born during the reign of King Herod the Great who, upon hearing a report of the birth of a new king, sought to kill him. Since Matthew states that Jesus was born before Herod the Great died, then Jesus must not have been born before 4 BC. Some have suggested a date closer to 7 BC. Perhaps the best that can be said is that Jesus was born sometime during the years 7 to 4 BC.

Even if the year of Jesus' birth could be determined, the month and day of Jesus' birth are unknown. Many early Christians thought it was not proper to celebrate Jesus' birth because such a celebration focuses on the human Jesus rather than on the spiritual and divine Christ. The earliest celebrations of Jesus' birth apparently took place in either April or May, which ironically is the same time that Easter is normally celebrated. However, eventually winter dates were established as the official date for Christmas. The eastern church (Orthodox or Greek Orthodox) established January 6 as the date of Christmas sometime in the 3rd or 4th centuries. In the west, the Roman Catholic Church identified December 25 in the 4th century.

Some have argued that if the priestly division of Abijah, of which Zechariah was a member (Luke 1:5), was scheduled to perform temple services in October, as some Jewish calendars may have indicated, then a December 25 date is possible. However, it has been suggested that since Luke records that there were shepherds out in the fields watching their flocks at the time of Jesus' birth, he may have been born in the springtime when the weather was warmer. If these flocks had been specifically bred for sacrifice in the Temple, the event could refer to virtually any day of the year. The point is there is no way to know, however, exactly when Jesus was born.

Luke's Version of the Birth of Jesus (Luke 2:1-20)

The trip to Bethlehem (Luke 2:1-7)

Luke indicates that the Roman emperor had decreed that a census of the empire's population be taken. In order to accomplish this, the heads of families were required to return to their ancestral home for registration. From a human perspective, then, Jesus was born in Bethlehem because of a Roman decree; yet Bethlehem was known as the city of David, the king. While Luke does not refer to the prophecy of Micah 5:2-4, he most likely expected his readers to conclude that Jesus' birth in Bethlehem was more than an accident of history, but part of God's plan. The journey from Nazareth of Galilee to Bethlehem of Judea was about 80 miles, and was accomplished while Mary was in her ninth month of pregnancy. After they arrived in Bethlehem, Joseph attempted to find a room but discovered that there were no more vacant rooms, because the census drew a large number of visitors, so Jesus was born in a stable. Caves were often utilized as stables, and that was probably true here. An important point is that Jesus was born in obscurity and in humility; this was not how the people at that time expected their promised king to come.

Honored by angels and shepherds (Luke 2:8-20)

Orthodox religious people considered shepherds unclean and simple-minded. They were suspected of not being truthful. Because they were considered basically dishonest people, shepherds were not allowed to testify in court. Significantly, the announcement of the birth of the Messiah was first given by the angels to shepherds, because it shows that God cares for people of all walks of life and that no one is unimportant to God.

The circumcision of Jesus and the presentation in the temple (Luke 2:21-40)

As faithful Jews who were careful to observe all the statutes of the Law of Moses, Joseph and Mary arranged to have Jesus circumcised at the required age of 8 days (Genesis 17:9-14; Exodus 12:44). Circumcision was the physical sign of the covenant, and perhaps was commanded of Jews because of God's promise to Abraham concerning his future descendants. After a waiting period of 41 days, known as Purification, Joseph and Mary brought the child to the priests in order to receive a blessing from the priest and to offer sacrifices. As evidence of their humble status, they offered two turtledoves--the least costly sacrificial animals allowed in the Mosaic Law (Leviticus 12:2-8).

The testimony of Anna and Simeon (Luke 2:25-40)

Luke's focus shifts to the testimonies of two old servants of God, Simeon and Anna. Simeon is called "a righteous and devout man" upon whom rested the Holy Spirit. In other words, he was a prophet who had been looking for the Messiah and had been assured that he would see him before he died. The saying, which comes from Simeon, was later named the 'Nunc

Dimmittis". In this oracle/song, Simeon declared that the Messiah would bring revelation to the Gentiles, meaning that he would be a universal savior. He also prophesied to Mary that a sword would pierce her heart, which probably is a reference to the suffering and death of Jesus. Anna the prophetess expresses thanksgiving to God and testifies to others that the child would bring about the ultimate redemption of Jerusalem.

Matthew's Version of the Birth of Christ (Matthew 2:1-23)

The visit of the wise men (Matthew 2:1-12)

Literally these men were called "magi." They were probably Persian astrologers. It is unknown what exactly caused them to search for a newborn king in Judea. Some believe that they had read astrological signs, which to them pointed to the birth of a new king. Others have suggested that they may have had some acquaintance with the Old Testament, which prophesied of a coming king. Perhaps they knew of the prophecy of Balaam in Numbers 24:17, which speaks of a star coming out of Jacob to set up his rule. While most scholars believe this originally referred to the rise of the kingdom of Israel and the great king David, it may have been interpreted in later times to have messianic significance.

Matthew records that when Herod heard the claims and inquiries of the magi he asked them where this new king was to be born and when the star was scheduled to appear. He also asked them to report back to him if and when they located the child and to report back to him concerning the child's whereabouts. But the narrative reveals the true motive of Herod behind this request of the magi. He was not seeking information to fill some curiosity, nor did he want to worship the newborn king. Rather, Herod's desire was to eliminate any possible threat to his throne. The text states that the magi followed the star, which led them to a manger in Bethlehem. Much has been made of the expensive gifts that the magi brought Jesus--that each gift had a spiritual significance or that three gifts suggests three magi. All of this is speculation, which gave fuel for legends which arose in later centuries surrounding both the gifts and the magi. What is more important is that the first people in Matthew's story to come and worship Jesus were Persian astrologers—Gentiles.

The flight to Egypt (Matthew 2:13-23)

Upon the instructions of an angel, Joseph, Mary, and Jesus fled to Egypt to escape the threat of Herod. Meanwhile, Herod ordered the death of all male children in Bethlehem who were two years or younger. As awful as that was, this was actually true to Herod's character. Secular history tells us that Herod killed some of his sons, one of his wives, and many trusted friends because of his desire to remain in power (*Antiquities of the Jews* 15.7.4-5; 16.11.7;17.2.4). The holy family stayed in Egypt until Herod's death, which probably took place after a relatively short period of time. After Herod's death, they first attempted to return to Bethlehem but were warned by an angel to go on to Galilee, to the city of Nazareth. Herod's son Archelaus was now ruler in Judea, and he was as ruthless as his father. Matthew 2:23 declares that the family's move to Nazareth was in fulfillment of prophecy, "He will be called a Nazarene." This passage does not appear in any known text of the Old Testament. Most scholars believe Matthew is making a play on words from the original Hebrew of Isaiah 11:1. "The Branch" in Hebrew is *Netzer,* which may sound similar to Nazarene.

The Childhood of Jesus (Luke 2:40-52)

The description in Luke of the physical, intellectual, and spiritual development of Jesus is almost exactly like that of the Old Testament prophet Samuel (1 Samuel 2:26), suggesting that Jesus also would carry out a prophet-type ministry. The only story in the gospels about the boy Jesus is found in Luke 2:41-50. In this story, a 12 year old Jesus is portrayed as discussing matters concerning the Law of Moses with the experts in the Law within the temple area. It is unknown whether there was a tradition at this time that when a boy reached the age of 12 he officially became a son of the covenant—a legal adult in relation to the Law of Moses. Jewish boys today are typically encouraged to go through a "Bar Mitzvah" service to express this adult status. The story indicates that on the return trip from Jerusalem, Jesus' parents realized that he had been missing for about 3 days. Eventually, Jesus was found in the temple discussing the

Law with the doctors or experts of the Law. The remarkable insight into the meaning of the Law which Jesus demonstrated in his conversation caused many to be amazed. His parents, however, were distraught over Jesus' being in the temple without their knowledge. Jesus' response to their rebuke provides a small glimpse into his nature. First, Jesus acknowledged God as his father. This was not typical. Most Jews believed that God was a heavenly father, but more a national and distant one than the personal and close father hinted at by Jesus. Second, his words suggest an early awareness of his special relationship with God as his Son. Third, the text implies that Jesus' parents should have known where he would be, since they supposedly knew who he was. Luke summarizes the next 18 years of Jesus' life by describing him as obedient to his parents and that he matured in every area of human life.

Chapter 4

The Baptism and Temptation of Jesus

This is the first episode in the life of Jesus where the synoptic gospels present common material. All three present an overview of the ministry of John the Baptist prior to a description of Jesus' baptism by John. In addition, all present John the Baptist in light of Isaiah 40, as the voice crying in the wilderness. Luke differs from Matthew and Mark by summarizing the political and religious leadership in the ancient middle east at the beginning of John's ministry.

The Political Situation

Luke notes that John was called by the Lord in the 15th year of the Emperor Tiberius (AD 15) at the time when Pontius Pilate was governor of Judea (AD 25-37). Herod Antipas was in power in Galilee (4 BC-AD 39), while Herod's brother Philip was in power in Iturea and Trachonitus (4 BC-AD 33). Luke also reports that John's call took place during the high priesthood of Annas and Caiaphas. Originally there was only one high priest, but under Roman rule, the high priest became more of a political position, often appointed by the Romans. Between the years 37 BC and AD 26, there were 28 different high priests. Annas had been high priest from AD 7 to 14. Caiaphas, who was Annas' son-in-law, succeeded him. But most likely Annas remained the power behind the office. In fact, the gospel of John states that when Jesus was arrested in Gethsemane, the first person he was taken to was Annas (John 18:12-14).

The Message of John (Matthew 3:1-12; Mark 1:1-8; Luke 3:3-18)

A Call for Repentance

The synoptics all state that the heart of John's message was a call for repentance because the kingdom of God would soon be upon them. The word "repentance" means to "turn" or "turn around," which is another way of saying "change your mind and your way of life." When a person repents, he or she acknowledges that his or her present way of living is wrong and desires God's forgiveness and the opportunity to start over again to live according to God's will. As both seal and symbol of one's repentance, John carried out a baptism of repentance for the forgiveness of sin. Repentance was necessary in order to be ready for the coming of the kingdom of God. According to Matthew, John attacked the notion that the Jews were secure in their hope for the Kingdom; rather, he asserted sin makes a people unprepared. The Pharisees and Sadducees were admonished to express genuine repentance because in their current condition they were nothing more than hypocrites.

In Luke 3:10-14, we find some specific ethical instructions which John gave to different groups. Within these instructions, which he gave in response to questions from each group, are basic moral teachings. In general, he called people to practice mercy and show personal concern for others. The ethical principles John exhorted the people to practice were not new. Rather, they are found in the Old Testament and thus constitute part of John's overall message of repentance. Not only did John condemn the Jewish people in general for sinfulness, he also publicly condemned Herod Antipas for his adulterous affair with Herodias, the former wife of his half brother Philip. For this bold statement, John was arrested and imprisoned (Luke 3:19-20).

The Announcement of the Imminent Kingdom of God and the Coming of the Messiah

In order to appreciate the importance of John's messages concerning the coming Kingdom of God, some explanations and definitions are in order. The term "kingdom" does not mean territory or political boundaries, nor does it imply any earthly political system. Instead, "kingdom" means "rule" or "sovereignty." Thus "the kingdom of God" has to do with God's rule wherever it may be found. As for human beings, it means the rule or sovereignty of God over the lives of the people and the world. John announced that God was about to dramatically break into human affairs to establish his rule. This event would involve the judgment and condemnation of sin and the sinner. In light of this, John called Israel to a radically different life style under the will of God. John's message of the kingdom of God looked forward with hope to the ultimate defeat of sin and the devil, and the establishment of the rule of God throughout the world.

John also spoke of the coming "someone," who was more powerful and worthy than he. Undoubtedly, John had in mind the Messiah. John said that this one will baptize with the Holy Spirit and fire. "Baptism of the Spirit" probably means spiritual cleansing, spiritual regeneration, new life. Matthew and Luke also have the phrase "baptism of fire," which probably refers to purification or judgment. According to John, this coming one will separate people, the good from the bad, as a farmer separates the wheat from the chaff, so the ministry of the Messiah will be that of salvation and judgment.

A Call to Baptism

As was mentioned above, John administered a baptism (i.e., immersion in water) in connection with people's repentance. In the ancient world, water rituals of some kind were known and practiced. The Jewish sect known as the Essenes practiced daily ceremonial washings for the purpose of spiritual purification. It used to be believed that John's baptism was an adaptation from the Jewish proselyte baptism (i.e., baptism of Gentile converts). When a Gentile would convert to Judaism, he or she would be required to undergo a baptism as a symbolic act of cleansing from past pagan ways and identity. If John had this in mind, then a call to baptism was required since Israel had become so spiritually corrupt that God no longer recognized them as his people, and they needed to be restored or "reconverted" through repentance and baptism. However, it is now widely accepted that there was no practice of proselyte baptism in the first century. More likely, John instituted the ritual of baptism as a new practice, drawing upon the widely understood significance of water rituals as acts of spiritual cleansing. Since it was an act of spiritual cleansing, the gospels describe it as a baptism unto repentance for the forgiveness of sins.

The Baptism of Jesus

Each gospel describes the baptism of Jesus, but with a different emphasis. Luke 3:21, for example, describes Jesus as one of the crowd who went to John for baptism and that his baptism was accompanied with prayer. On the other hand, Matthew 3:13-17 stresses that John was hesitant to baptize Jesus because he recognized Jesus as superior to him. Matthew apparently desired to address a concern that some Christians had expressed concerning Jesus' baptism—the Christian belief in the divine nature of Jesus. Matthew may have heard the concern expressed in this way: "If John baptized for repentance for the forgiveness of sins, why was Jesus baptized? If it is true that Jesus was sinless, then why did he desire to be baptized?" Through the years, many answers have been suggested. The simplest and most obvious answer is what Jesus said in Matthew 3:15. "Let it be so now; for it is proper for us in this way to fulfill all righteousness." This means Jesus desired to do all that God requires. Thus it was an act of simple obedience to God. But scholars believe there may have been more involved in Jesus' decision to be baptized than what is stated in Matthew. Here are two theories:

1. He may have been baptized in preparation for the coming of the kingdom.
2. He may have been baptized in order to identify with the people. Even though he was the Son of God, he was not relieved of the responsibility which all people have. He shows that he can identify

with experiences of others. Also, by being baptized, he identified with the people in their quest for deliverance from the stain and guilt of sin.

The Approval of God

The gospels state that after Jesus was baptized he received divine approval for his action. Each gospel notes that the heavens opened (Mark said the heavens were torn apart). The scene is more than simply "there was a break in the clouds and the sun was seen in all of its brilliance." Rather, the reader is to imagine the very doors of heaven were being opened. Or, as Mark puts it, the spiritual curtain that separates humankind from God was torn open so that Jesus could hear and perhaps directly encounter God himself. Also, with heaven open, the Holy Spirit descended upon Jesus. Like a bird or, more specifically, a dove let out of a cage, the Holy Spirit comes to earth and rests on Jesus. Matthew and Mark state that the spirit descended "like a dove," with no clear implication that this descent was a visual or physical event. Luke, however, says that the spirit had a bodily form, although he does not specify that the bodily form was that of a dove. The importance of this event is that it signified the moment of Jesus' divine anointing. This experience served as a kind of inauguration of Jesus' messianic and prophetic ministry. From this point on, Jesus was truly the anointed one, which is the meaning of the title "Messiah."

After the Holy Spirit came upon him, the gospels all record that a voice from heaven declared that Jesus is God's son, with whom God is well pleased. According to Mark and Luke, the voice spoke directly to Jesus: "You are my Son." However, in Matthew the voice spoke to someone(s) other than Jesus saying: "This is my Son." Most likely, God spoke directly to Jesus. Perhaps Matthew reworded the saying in order for the reader to understand that in reality God is calling to them through this gospel to come to faith in Jesus. Actually the sentence "You are (this is) my beloved son" is a partial quotation from Psalm 2:7. Psalm 2 is a royal or coronation psalm. It was originally written to honor the newly-crowned king of Israel. The fact that this is said of Jesus leads us to conclude that God is affirming Jesus not only as his Son, but as the newly chosen King. The phrase "with whom I am well pleased" is a partial quote from Isaiah 42:1.

Isaiah 42 is one of several chapters in the latter part of Isaiah which have been designated "Servant Songs" because the writer is extolling someone(s) called "the servant of the Lord." The last servant song is Isaiah 53, in which the servant suffers and dies for the sins of the nation. The "servant of the Lord" is an individual (or collectively the people of Israel) whose entire mission is to do the will of God by serving God and others. Perhaps God was indicating that Jesus' divine sonship and Messiahship would be exercised through service and suffering instead of power and glory.

The Temptation of Jesus (Matthew 4:1-11, Mark 1:12-13, Luke 4:1-13)

Preliminary observations

Before examining the account of the temptation of Jesus in the desert, preliminary observations must be made. First, the gospels connect the temptation account with the baptism of Jesus. In both, the concept of Jesus as God's son is found. At his baptism, God declared Jesus to be the Son, while during the temptation the devil raised some questions concerning this divine sonship. The devil's statement, typically translated from the original Greek, "If you are the son of God," should probably be translated, "since you are the son of God." If the devil's words are read as "since you are …," rather than "if you are ...," then the devil's agenda was really about the nature of Jesus' sonship rather than the truth of this claim. Thus, the temptation of Jesus was concerned with the nature of the ministry of Jesus—how Jesus would conduct himself as the Son of God.

Second, the temptations of Jesus were real temptations. If Jesus had been protected from sin, there would not have been any possibility of sin. If that were true, Jesus would not have really been really tempted. A temptation is only real when the subject is truly vulnerable. If Jesus had only pretended to be tempted, or if God had arranged it so Jesus could not have sinned, then this story has little value for humans. If, however, Jesus had been truly tempted and chose to resist and remain obedient, then he became for humanity a powerful example of one who chose the right and rejected the wrong.

The temptations were actually a test. The Greek word for temptation can also mean "trials" or "test." The Holy Spirit sent Jesus into the desert to be tempted so that he might undergo testing by the devil. In his typical dramatic style, Mark states that the Spirit "drove" or "cast" out Jesus into the wilderness to be tempted. The point is not that God was trying to seduce Jesus to sin, but rather to test him in order that his true character might be seen.

The Temptations

Mark only records that Jesus was in the wilderness for forty days and was tempted by Satan, but says nothing about the nature of those temptations. The fuller version of the temptation story is found in Matthew and Luke, who tell the same story but in a slightly different manner. Both Matthew and Luke describe the three temptations the same way: turning stones into bread, leaping from the pinnacle of the temple, falling down and worshipping Satan in order to receive the kingdoms of the world. But the order of the temptations is different. Matthew's order is: (1) stones, (2) temple, (3) worship Satan. Luke's order is: (1) stones, (2) worship Satan, (3) temple. This seemingly insignificant difference may reveal a different agenda for both gospels. The movement of Matthew's story is from the desert, to Jerusalem, to a high mountain. Mountains, especially high mountains are important for Matthew, perhaps because Jesus is compared to Moses, who received God's law on the mountain. On the other hand, in Luke the movement of the story is from the desert, to someplace up, presumably a mountain, to Jerusalem. And Jerusalem is very important in Luke as the place where the Messiah was rejected and killed. Whatever the significance, the following analysis will follow Matthew's account.

The First Temptation: Stones to Bread

In the first temptation, the tempter suggests to Jesus that he turn some stones into bread. Since Matthew points out that Jesus had been fasting for 40 days and was very hungry, the reader can appreciate Jesus' dilemma. Probably this was a temptation for Jesus to use his power selfishly. It is commonly understood that Jesus was being tempted to satisfy his hunger and thus avoid the hardship of fasting. Others, however, have suggested that this was also a temptation to use his power as a means to win followers. One common belief was that the Messiah would end hunger. But Jesus' response reveals he had a higher priority than simply taking care of human needs. His words point out that material needs are not the deepest needs of people. Spiritual needs are more important. Jesus would not take the easy way, nor avoid his suffering; rather, he would trust in God to sustain him. It is interesting to note that Jesus' words are a quote from Deuteronomy 8:3. The context of this passage is that Moses was reminding the people how God tested them in the wilderness for forty years in order that they might learn to trust in the very word of God.

The Second Temptation: Leap from the Temple to Invoke God's Protection

Then the devil took Jesus to Jerusalem, placed him on the top of the temple, and suggested that he leap from the pinnacle of the temple in order to show God would protect him from getting hurt. This may have been a temptation to sensationalism. There was a popular rabbinical belief that the Messiah would come by appearing dramatically out of heaven and on top of the temple (*Peskita Rabba* 162a). In an early Christian writing, the heretic Simon Magus (Simon the Sorcerer of Acts 8:9-24) claimed to be able to leap from mountains and not be killed or injured (*Pseudo-Clementine Recognitions* 2:9). It may also have been a test of Jesus' willingness to trust God in all situations, no matter how risky or dangerous. Perhaps the devil was suggesting that Jesus should test God's faithfulness to him by forcing him to protect him from harm. In order to prove his point, the devil quoted Psalm 91:11-12. He did not, however, cite Psalm 91:9-10,14, in which the promise is only given to those who are totally trusting in and committed to God.

In response, Jesus again quoted from the book of Deuteronomy (6:16). Based on this text, Jesus reminded the devil that for one to test God's word amounted to a lack of faith. If one were to throw himself into danger in order for God to protect him miraculously, the action is not faith; instead, it is presumption and arrogance. In contrast to this, Jesus understood that he was called to trust and obey God's will with the assurance of the resources and strength he would need to accomplish his mission.

The Third Temptation: Worship Satan to Receive the Kingdoms of the World

The third temptation is the most difficult of all the temptations to understand, because it appears that the temptation to fall down and worship Satan would be no temptation at all. Who would willingly submit to Satan? Perhaps this temptation can best be understood as a temptation to compromise. The text acknowledges the devil's position and that he has considerable possessions. Perhaps the compromise has to do with an interest in the kingdoms of the world instead of the kingdom of God. The former is earthly, and the latter is heavenly and spiritual. Such a compromise would involve a different conception of his ministry as the Messiah. Instead of preaching and healing in order to usher in the spiritual kingdom of God, Jesus would take on the role of a military messiah and fight against the earthly forces such as the Romans. In contrast to war, Jesus understood that he had been called to serve and suffer.

Jesus' response to Satan is a reaffirmation of the basic principle for people who calls themselves servants of God. That principle is that only God is to be worshipped and honored, and only God is to be served. With this answer, Jesus refused to compromise with Satan; moreover, Satan is totally rejected and opposed, but Jesus also rejected the popular Messianic view of military hero. Rather, he chose the uncompromising path of teaching and service as his mission.

Jesus and temptations

In review of Jesus and his response to the devil's temptations, what lessons are there for Christian as we seek to follow the example of Jesus in daily living? First, Jesus knew and used the scripture in each repudiation of the temptation. He understood that the written word of God is a valuable resource for spiritual development. Within the Bible, one not only learns the commands of God, but also the failures and successes of the people of God, which can serve as warnings and inspirations for believers today. Second, Jesus' victory over temptation reflects his trust in God to provide for his needs and well being. Jesus understood that the attractiveness of the easy and popular way is not always the right or best way. Rather, even when it doesn't make sense according to conventional wisdom, he can rest assured that God's way is best.

Luke states explicitly what Matthew implies: that the temptations of Jesus did not end with this event. Jesus had won the first round, and the devil left Jesus to plan for the next contest or until another opportune time. In fact, it may be that Jesus' greatest temptation would come later, in the garden and on the cross.

Chapter 5

Jesus' Early Galilean Ministry

Summary of early ministry of Jesus in Galilee (Mark 1:14-15, Matthew 4:12-17, Luke 4:14-15)

Sometime after Jesus' baptism and temptation, the gospels record that he left for Galilee to begin his ministry. The exact chronology of events and the time in which Jesus began his prophetic work is somewhat unclear. Matthew and Mark state that Jesus went to Galilee preaching the gospel after the arrest of John the Baptist. Thus assuming the chronology of Matthew and Mark, Jesus' ministry began as John's ended. Mark, stresses that Jesus preached the good news of God, which was the message of the fulfillment of God's promises to Israel, the nearness of the Kingdom, and the call for repentance and faith. Matthew, however, stresses the prophetic significance of Jesus' early ministry--that his ministry was in fulfillment of prophecy. Matthew also notes that Jesus made his home in Capernaum, which was located near a great number of villages on or near the shore of the Sea of Galilee so that over 100,000 people could easily reach the city by either foot or boat. For Luke, the important characteristic of Jesus' early ministry was his power and popularity. In fact, Luke states that Jesus returned to Galilee "with the power of the Holy Spirit."

Jesus at Nazareth/His sermon and rejection by the townspeople (Luke 4:16-30)

Matthew and Mark place Jesus' visit to Nazareth and the subsequent rejection as having occurred in the second or third years of his ministry (Matthew 13:54-58; Mark 6:1-6a). However, Luke's account places the same event near the very beginning of Jesus' ministry. While Matthew and Mark may have preserved the original historical context for this story, Luke apparently has placed this narrative in a different chronological setting. If it is possible to determine the reason for artificially changing the setting, it may be that, for Luke, what Jesus said at Nazareth was particularly fitting as a kind of theme statement for his ministry. For Luke, Jesus' Nazareth sermon was an inaugural sermon, not in the sense that this sermon officially launched his ministry, but that the ideas of the sermon effectively describe Jesus' practice and understanding of the goals of his ministry. This overview will follow Luke and review this sermon in light of how he fulfilled his prophetic ministry. However, before this analysis, a brief summary of synagogue worship is required.

The setting for synagogue worship

In a typical synagogue worship service, people were segregated by gender. The men sat in the main room, while the women and children stood or sat behind some kind of partition. The Scriptures, which were in scroll form, were contained in a painted wooden box called an Ark. There was a pulpit or podium for the reader and interpreter of the Scriptures. A typical ancient synagogue worship service included the following in this order:

1. Singing from the Psalms
2. Recitation of the Shema (Deuteronomy 6:4-9)
3. Recitation of the prayers, called the 18 Benedictions
4. Reading a passage from the Law (Torah) and then from the prophets. Usually the reader would pause between verses in order to permit the interpreters to translate and interpret the verse from the ancient Hebrew to the contemporary Aramaic. Often everyone stood while the Scriptures were read.

5. Delivering the sermon. It was customary for the synagogue leader to invite a visiting rabbi to deliver the sermon. The teacher/preacher usually sat down to preach.

Jesus' sermon

A Jubilee Sermon?

When Jesus got up to speak in his home synagogue, he apparently deliberately chose the passage in Isaiah to be read. The text was Isaiah 61:1-2 along with a line from Isaiah 58:6. In its original context, Isaiah 61 was concerned about the liberation of Israel from exile. However, this text was widely regarded as a messianic prophecy. More importantly, in Jesus' day this text was associated with the celebration of Jubilee (see Deuteronomy 15:1-2 and Leviticus 25:8-13). Jubilee was a holy season in the Jewish calendar, which occurred every 50 years. The heart of Jubilee was the cancellation of debts, emancipation of slaves, and the return of lost land and all other property to the original owner. According to Leviticus 25, a trumpet was to be blown at the start of Jubilee and liberty was to be declared throughout the land. It is highly unlikely that Jesus' ministry began at the start of Jubilee, nor was he setting up a new date for Jubilee. Jesus may have spiritually interpreted the contents of the passage to simply refer to the messianic age; other Jews may have also done this. But it may also describe something about the nature of Jesus' ministry—a ministry to the outcast and dispossessed of society. Thus this is also a message of deliverance.

A Compassionate Ministry

The focus of Jesus' sermon was on himself and his ministry. Quoting from Isaiah 61, he announced that he had been anointed with the Spirit. Most likely he was referring to his baptism and the dove which came upon him. Because he had been anointed, he can claim to be the Messiah. Jesus also claimed that he had been given a ministry of compassion and deliverance to the outcasts of society, to preach the good news to the poor, and to obtain the release of the prisoners. Jesus was called to be a healer of the blind and the liberator of the oppressed. He is to proclaim the year of the Lord's favor, the age of salvation, the age of the messiah.

The reaction of the people was mixed. Many were impressed and amazed, while others apparently expressed doubt. Jesus responded to their mixed reaction by rebuking their unbelief. He cited a proverb about a physician and then accused them of wanting him to perform a miracle in order to prove himself to them. In other words, their hearts were not open to the testimony of Scripture and others. After that, he quoted a second proverb which said that prophets are usually not accepted by the people from their home town, a stinging rebuke of the people of Nazareth.

Then Jesus gave two illustrations from the Old Testament, from which he argued that even the prophets of old sometimes ministered to Gentiles. He referred to the Old Testament stories concerning the widow of Zarephath and of Naaman the Syrian. Jesus noted that Elijah miraculously helped the widow of Zarephath to obtain food during a severe famine. She was a Gentile and the only one that Elijah helped at that time (1 Kings 17:8-16). He reminded the people that Elisha responded to the request of the Syrian general Naaman by healing him of his leprosy. This was the only leper Elisha healed at that time (2 Kings 5:1-5). Jesus was probably implying that the prophets only helped these Gentiles because there was no faith in Israel. With these stories, Jesus had reserved his most shocking words until the end of his brief speech. Here he revealed the universal nature of his mission. He warned them of what he would do if they, along with the rest of Israel, rejected him. Their rejection of Jesus would lead to the reaching out to the Gentiles. The term "gentile" comes from the Greek word for "nation" or "nations." It was an all-inclusive term to refer to all people who are not a part of the people of Israel; in other words, everyone who is not a Jew. The Greek word comes from the ancient Hebrew word, which is typically translated as "the nations." Gentiles were considered by Jews as ceremonially unclean, immoral, and ungodly. Thus it was generally considered unwise to have much association with Gentiles. What was particularly upsetting to nearly all Jews was that they and their lands were controlled by the Gentiles, i.e., the Romans.

The crowds understood the meaning of Jesus' words and became enraged. They opposed any thought of reaching out to Gentiles and understood Jesus' implied accusation of their faithlessness. The crowd was so angry, in fact, that they left the synagogue in a mob to kill Jesus, but he was able to pass through them without being harmed.

Jesus' Nazareth sermon is important because it lays before the reader some of the most important characteristics of his ministry, which, by extension, are to be characteristics of his followers. First, Jesus understood himself to be a messiah of compassion and deliverance to the helpless and rejected. He was the "Servant Messiah." Second, Jesus understood himself to be a messiah for all people, both Jew and Gentile--He was the "Universal Messiah." Third, Jesus also understood himself to be a messiah that would suffer rejection by his own people. He was the "Suffering Messiah."

The Call of the first disciples (Matthew 4:18-22, Mark 1:16-20, Luke 5:1-11)

Matthew and Mark portray the first calling as if Jesus came along and surprisingly challenged Peter, Andrew, James, and John to leave their fathers' fishing business and follow him on his journey. The emphasis was on the urgency of the moment and the challenge to make a decision now. Luke, however, describes the calling in the context of a preaching ministry of Jesus and the subsequent miracle of the great catch of fish. According to Luke, Jesus had been preaching in Simon Peter's boat. He did this in order to escape the crowd which had been pressing in on him. After the sermon, Jesus commanded Peter to put out to sea in order to catch fish. Simon (Peter) pointed out to Jesus that he and his crew had worked all through the night without any success, but he agreed to go out and try again. This time, their efforts were successful. In fact, the catch of fish was so great that men from other boats came over to help pull the nets up.

Luke also points out that when Simon realized that a miracle had just taken place, he bowed before Jesus in fear, and asked him to depart because he was a sinner. However, Jesus pointed out that the great catch of fish was more than a miracle, but a sign that Jesus would make these men and women to become fishers of people. Luke concludes this narrative with the note that the men left everything and followed Jesus.

Chapter 6

Miracles in the Ministry of Jesus

Introduction to the miracles of Jesus

Definition of a miracle

The story of the great catch of fish is one of many miracle stories found in the gospel record. But what exactly is a miracle? One popular definition is that a miracle is something which is usually impossible to do. Thus, if it is impossible to walk on water, then to walk on water would be a miracle. Yet science and technology have changed our understanding of what is, or what is not, impossible. A hundred years ago, it would have been considered impossible to fly to the moon; but, of course, that "miracle" took place in 1969. Perhaps the word "impossible" is too limiting, since we have not yet determined the limits of human achievement.

Closely related to this concept, others have defined a miracle as something which violates the laws of nature. Yet, again, these laws are really categories imposed by science. But has humanity learned all the laws of the universe? Perhaps there might be conditions in which the universe is not merely so fixed and explainable as first believed.

Whatever scientific definition best suits the word miracle, the fact is that the New Testament does not discuss miracles from the perspective of science, but from the perspective of faith in God. The three most important words found in the New Testament that refer to a miracle are words of faith and not scientific description. These words are:

1. "Miracle" or, more literally, "mighty work." This word highlights a work Jesus did which demonstrates God's mighty power.
2. "Wonders." This refers to works which evoke some kind of response of awe or amazement by those who witnessed the miracle.
3. "Sign." This interprets the works of Jesus to have some spiritual meaning beyond the obvious visual and physical result of the miracle. For example, in Matthew 12:28, Jesus said: "But if it is by the Spirit of God that I cast out demons, then the kingdom of God has come to you." Jesus' point was that his ability to cast out demons was not only evidence that Jesus has supernatural power, but that the rule of God through the work of Jesus has begun to invade and take control of the realm of Satan. So the miracle pointed to the kingdom of God.

Types of miracles

The gospels describe four general types of miracles by Jesus.

1. Miracles of Healing: fever, leprosy, paralysis, dumbness, atrophy, hemorrhage, deafness, speech impediment, blindness, epilepsy, infirmity, dropsy, severed ear.
2. Miracles of Nature: stilling the storm, feeding the multitude, walking on water, cursing the fig tree, turning water into wine.
3. Exorcism: casting out evil spirits or demons from a person.
4. Resurrections: Jairus' daughter, the widow's son, Lazarus.

Characteristics of Jesus' miracles

When one examines the miracles of Jesus, it is possible to detect some general characteristics. First, the gospels portray the miracles as genuine historical events. Second, they were almost always done by Jesus to meet some human need. Third, Jesus' miracles were generally performed openly, before many spectators, and in a variety of situations. Fourth, Jesus healed people instantly. He did it without the use of some special incantation or ritual, and by merely speaking the word of healing to someone. And fifth, the miracles were understood by Jesus as the signs of the dawn of the Messianic Age. They were evidence that the kingdom of God was breaking into human existence.

Purpose of the miracles of Jesus

The question "Why did Jesus perform miracles?" may seem to have an obvious answer. Perhaps the common explanation for the miracles of Jesus is that they were done to confirm the claim that Jesus was, in fact, the Messiah, the Son of God. But the gospel also tells us that Jesus had other reasons. For example, according to Matthew 12:28, miracles were done to demonstrate that the power and rule of God was overcoming the power and rule of Satan. Moreover, it also seems to be true that Jesus performed miracles simply to reveal the power and love of God. While Jesus understood the importance of his ministry and the role of miracles within it, he did not consider a faith which rested primarily on miracles to be the right kind of faith; in fact, he condemned such faith. As valuable as miracles were for Jesus, they appear to have been of secondary importance compared to his work of preaching and teaching. As noted above, sometimes Jesus healed someone simply because he cared for that person. He saw miracles as the evidence of the power of God at work.

Jesus' early Galilean ministry of preaching and healing

Jesus in the synagogue at Capernaum (Mark 1:21-28, Luke 4:31-37)

One of the first places visited by Jesus in his Galilean ministry was the city of Capernaum. According to Luke, Capernaum had a synagogue which had been built with the financial assistance of a Roman centurion (Luke 7:2-5). Mark and Luke recorded that Jesus went to Capernaum at the beginning of his Galilean ministry and on the sabbath attended the synagogue. Apparently, Jesus had been invited to give a lesson to the people, for the gospels state that the people were impressed with the authority of Jesus' teaching. Most rabbis followed the practice of citing the Rabbinical traditions and interpretations of the Bible, thus pointing to the authority of another. In contrast, Jesus spoke as the authority, and this authority seemed to come from him. Jesus' personal authority was vividly demonstrated by casting out an evil spirit from a man simply by a word of command. The people in the synagogue were absolutely amazed at this and said among themselves, "What is this? A new teaching—with authority! He commands even the unclean spirits and they obey him" (Mark 1:27).

Special Topic: Demonology in the New Testament

Demon possession is mentioned only twice in the Old Testament and twice in the New Testament (after the gospels). Compared to other first-century non-Christian literature, demon possession and exorcisms are considerably rare in the Bible. The gospels portray demon possession as a separate malady from other problems, though physical and behavioral disorders can accompany it. Jesus is consistently shown as one who had complete authority over the demons. He merely had to speak a word of command and the demon would respond. This authority over the spirits continues in the early church with the ministry of the apostles and others.

The healing of Peter's mother-in-law (Matthew 8:14-15, Mark 1:29-31, Luke 4:38-39)

All three gospels present an account of the healing of Peter's mother-in-law. One minor point of interest is that Peter is shown to be married (see Paul's reference to the marital status of Peter [Cephas] in 1 Corinthians 9:5). Matthew and Mark stress that the healing of Peter's mother-in-law resulted by the healing touch of Jesus. In their account, the healing power of Jesus is clearly seen. Luke, however, stresses that Jesus "rebuked" the fever, as he might a person or an evil spirit (Luke 5:34-35). Note the authority of Jesus. It may be that Luke wants his readers to understand that Jesus' healing of disease is not all that much different from the casting out of an evil spirit and that illnesses were part of living under the rule of the devil. Like the exorcisms, the healing miracles were a demonstration of God's power and authority entering into the world. Luke also added that the healing was instantaneous, showing even more vividly the power of Jesus over disease.

Summary of other healings (Mark 1:32-38, Luke 4:40-43)

In addition to the specific miracle stories, the gospels sometimes present summaries of Jesus' ministry of healing and exorcism. For the second time, both Mark and Luke mention that the exorcised demons recognized Jesus as the Holy One of God. Jesus, however, commanded them to be silent. Most scholars are convinced that the gospels, especially Mark, emphasized Jesus' desire to keep his true identity secret during his ministry. This is commonly referred to as the m*essianic secret.* Scholars suggest that the gospel writer must have had some literary or theological reason for stressing Jesus' messianic secret. Yet, if the gospels are a narrative of what Jesus actually did, then why did he keep quiet about his special identity? One reason, drawn from the gospels themselves, is that Jesus sought some privacy for the purpose of prayer, but the constant demands of the crowds for healing made this very difficult. Thus Jesus may have been concerned that the people had become so enamored with his miracles that they had lost sight of the real purpose of his ministry. Jesus wanted the people to know that his real ministry was to preach. However, the irony is that Jesus' popularity actually increased because of his healing ministry.

Healing a leper (Matthew 8:1-4, Mark 1:40-45, Luke 5:12-16)

Mark and Luke next record Jesus' healing of a leper. Matthew places this story before the healing of Peter's mother-in-law, and these, along with other miracles, are placed after the Sermon on the Mount (Matthew 5-7).

Leprosy and the ancient Jew

Leprosy was a defiling and dirty disease to the Jews. The biblical word for leprosy can actually refer to several kinds of skin diseases from minor conditions, such as psoriasis, to full blown leprosy (*elephantias graecorum*). Many people believed that leprosy was a direct punishment from God for serious sins. Victims of leprosy were to be shunned by everyone else because people feared that they also could be infected. More importantly, perhaps, most people regarded the disease as ritually unclean; so anyone who had close contact with a leper could also become unclean. Consequently, the leper was required to live apart from normal society. They usually wore torn clothing and loose hair as a sign of their disease; and with covered mouth, a leper was supposed to cry out "Unclean, unclean" to those who might pass his way. According to the Mosaic Law, a leper would remain in a state of uncleanness until he was pronounced "clean" by the priest.

The healing of the leper

The text states that the leper approached Jesus to ask for help. This was in direct violation of the Jewish custom. Upon hearing the man's request, Jesus was moved with pity. All the gospels point out that Jesus touched the man. With this action Jesus violated the taboo, for by touching an unclean object or person one becomes unclean. The touch of Jesus appears to have been a touch of empathy. In some sense, he shared in the leper's defilement. Jesus' action was a visible sign of his compassion and acceptance toward even the most despicable. As with Peter's mother-in-law, the man was healed instantly.

Jesus then sternly charged the man not to tell anyone what happened. The phrase, "sternly charged" can actually mean "angrily warned." Why would Jesus be angry? Perhaps he did not want to be known as a faith healer and thought that this miracle could hamper his ministry. Assuming that Jesus knew that the leper would not obey Jesus' words, but would tell others, and that this would lead to the spreading of reports of this miracle throughout Galilee, Jesus may have been angry because he knew what was going to happen. Whatever the truth is, the leper did not keep silent about his healing, the news did spread throughout Galilee, and, consequently, Jesus' ministry was hampered.

Chapter 7

Controversies and Questions

This chapter will examine stories in which Jesus' teachings or works caused controversy or generated questions. These stories appear together as if they were grouped together. All three synoptic gospels place these stories after a collection of miracle stories. Most likely the gospel writers either drew from some early Christian collection of miracle stories and controversy stories, or one of the gospels, probably Mark, arranged these stories in groups.

The healing of the paralytic (Matthew 9:1-9, Mark 2:1-12, Luke 5:17-26)

While the story of the healing of the paralytic is about a miracle of Jesus, it is really a controversy story, for connected with the miracle is Jesus' claim to have the authority to forgive sins. The story opens with Jesus back in Capernaum, possibly at Peter's home. Along with Jesus and the disciples, present were scribes and Pharisees who apparently wanted to examine the work of Jesus. This is the first time when a close investigation by the religious leaders took place. Four friends sought access to Jesus on behalf of a sick man. The large crowd at the entrance and inside made it impossible for the men to carry their friend to Jesus. Refusing to be discouraged, the four friends eventually climbed on top of the house and lowered their friend through the roof of the house. Now it should be noted that Palestinians generally had flat roofs. The roof was often used like an upper porch. Often, there was an outside stairway to the roof. The roof would have been easy to dig through since between the beams was a covering of packed reeds and branches, covered with mortar and topped with earth.

When Jesus first sees the man, he forgives the man of his sins before healing him. Somehow Jesus connected sin and sickness. Some have suggested that the paralyzed man was actually in this condition because of guilt of a past sin. However, this is sheer speculation. Others have suggested that Jesus wanted to make a connection between sin and sickness--that people live in a fallen world, in which sin and sickness are closely related.

Jesus' critics objected to his words because they understood that only God can truly forgive sins. Thus Jesus, by saying these words, was claiming the right to forgive sin. More than that, Jesus was virtually saying that he was divine. Before the healing, Jesus asked the crowd, "Which is easier," to heal or forgive? Then he demonstrated his power to forgive by healing the man.

The call of Levi (Matthew 9:9-13, Mark 2:13-17, Luke 5:27-32)

Special Topic: Tax collecting in the Roman Empire

One of the ways that the Roman government collected taxes was by farming out the task. They would assess a district a certain amount and then sell the right to collect the taxes to the highest bidder. Romans only cared that the right amount of tax was collected. Any money above the required amount would be considered as profit for the collector--sort of a fee for services rendered or a commission for taxes collected. The people had no way of knowing what the property tax was supposed to be because it was completely under the control of the tax collectors. Consequently, the people, especially the Jewish populace, associated tax collectors with thieves and murderers. Moreover, Jewish tax collectors were considered by other Jews as traitors to the nation of Israel.

The call of Levi

Jesus called Levi (the gospel of Matthew named this tax collector Matthew) to follow him as a disciple—Levi responded by leaving his entire business. After he decided to follow Jesus, Levi invited Jesus to dine with him and his friends, whom Mark called tax collectors and sinners. Luke described this occasion as a great banquet. It may have been a kind of farewell banquet in anticipation of Levi's new life as a disciple of Jesus. Middle Eastern culture considered the act of eating a meal in another person's house as an act of friendship and acceptance for one another. Thus, Jesus was acting in such a way that extended friendship to everyone in the house, especially to Levi.

The Pharisees, however, objected to Jesus associating with people of such low reputation. In response, Jesus said that he went to these people because they had needs, like a doctor who goes to attend to the ill. When Jesus said, "Those who are well have no need of a physician," he was not suggesting that there were some who were truly well and needed no healing. Rather, Jesus was seeking to change the perspective of the Pharisees who habitually avoided the sinners and the needy. Jesus then quoted from Hosea 6:6 where the prophet sought to remind Israel that true religion is more than a rigid keeping of the rules. Instead it is a way of life by which the believer seeks to extend mercy to others. With this, Jesus showed his commitment to be a friend to the lost, the needy, the immoral, and the despised.

The question of fasting (Matthew 9:14-17, Mark 2:18-22, Luke 5:33-39)

The synoptic gospels place this incident immediately after the dinner at Matthew's house, yet some time lapse must be assumed. It is highly doubtful Jesus would have been encountered by the disciples of John the Baptist or the Pharisees at a tax collector's house, especially where there were other tax collectors and sinners. Some people, then, associated with the disciples of John the Baptist and the Pharisees asked Jesus about fasting. At this time, John the Baptist was in prison. The question that was raised was why Jesus and his disciples did not practice the fasts and prayers as other Jews did.

Special Topic: The practice of fasting and Jewish tradition

The Mosaic Law required people to fast only once per year on the Day of Atonement. Later, Jewish tradition required fasting twice every week, normally on Monday and Thursday (Luke 18:12, Megillat Taanit 12a). Fasting was usually connected with prayers which were offered at fixed times every day. For some, fasting became a display—whitened faces and torn clothing (Matthew 6:16-18). For some Jews, fasting may have been viewed as another burden of religion which, if faithfully performed, could help earn merit with God. Others, perhaps the disciples of John, may have fasted as a sign or warning of impending judgment unless there was repentance.

Criticism and response

Jesus' willingness to associate with people of questionable reputation and yet not regularly observe the traditional fasts was offensive to certain religious leaders. To them, Jesus was guilty of ignoring accepted religious practice and often behaving in ways that appeared to them to be in total disregard of the accepted interpretations of the Law.

Jesus responded to their questions and criticisms through metaphors and parables. First, he observed that no one is sad at a wedding feast for a wedding feast always suggests celebration. The point Jesus was making was that he is the bridegroom and his ministry is a type of wedding feast. In the Old Testament prophetic literature, God is often described as the bridegroom and Israel is his bride. Later, the coming "Messianic Age" was described as a wedding feast. Sadness occurs only when the bridegroom is taken away, a probable reference to his death.

Along with this metaphor, the gospels include Jesus' parable of the unshrunken cloth and wine skins. It is not clear whether or not Jesus originally told this parable in connection with his comments about the bridegroom and wedding feast. Since the lesson is very compatible, though, with that of the bridegroom and wedding, it was appropriate for early Christians to bring them together. It was common practice for the poor to patch clothing. Everyone knew that an unshrunken cloth would tear an old cloth after a washing. Similarly, it is obvious that new wine in old brittle wine skins will burst the skins--new wine needs new skins. Most likely the old clothes and the old wine represents the old approach to piety by the Pharisees and John the Baptist. The new garment and the new wine represent the new way of Jesus. The point of the parable seems to be that the way of Jesus is so totally different from the old ways that it cannot be forced into the old forms or traditions. Jesus did not come to reform Judaism, but to usher in a new age. Yet if one tries to force Jesus into the mold of the Pharisees or John, then as the old garment and the old skins were destroyed along with the new cloth and new wine, so both the old and the new ways of faith will be destroyed. The new way of Jesus demands a new tradition. While this new tradition of Jesus shares some elements in common with the tradition of the Pharisees, the differences are so great that the two cannot be combined. Thus the parable showed that Jesus as Messiah is the bringer of the era of joy and celebration. He is also the bringer of a totally new era.

Controversy over the Sabbath Law (Matthew 12:1-4, Mark 2:23-3:6, Luke 6:1-11)

Special Topic: History of the Sabbath tradition and the oral law

The Old Testament Law commanded the Jews to observe the sabbath for at least three reasons. First, the sabbath was to be kept to honor God, who rested after creating the world in 6 days. This was a day to be kept holy to God, which meant it was to be a day of worship. Second, keeping the sabbath was to help the Jews remember their own bondage in Egypt, where it was not possible to find rest from one's labor. Third, the sabbath was to be a day of rest. Being free from the normal busy routine of life, people are free to concentrate on God and family, and find physical and spiritual renewal.

By Jesus' time, the Mosaic Law, including the sabbath legislation, was modified with oral tradition. Many Jews believed that God gave the oral law at the same time he gave the written law to Moses. The oral law was given in order that the Law could be a dynamic reality, able to adapt to the changing needs and circumstances of the people. Furthermore, the oral law could actually help prevent people from breaking the written law by providing stricter guidelines than found in the written code. The Rabbis often referred to the oral law as the fence around the Law. The purpose, then, of the oral law was to help keep Israel from transgressing it.

With respect to the sabbath day, the Pharisees believed that one must keep the traditions as well as the Law itself. The vastness of the oral law can be seen in the later collections and codified editions of the traditions.

1. In 200 AD the oral law was collected and codified in written form in a volume known as the Mishnah.
2. Around 400-500 AD, further collections and codifications of the oral law were written. In addition to the Mishnah, the later rabbinical commentary on the Mishnah itself was collected in what has become a multi-volume work known as the Talmud. There are two Talmuds, the Jerusalem Talmud and the preferred and much longer Babylonian Talmud.

The oral tradition concerning the sabbath is itself quite extensive. In the Mishnah, about 24 chapters are devoted to the sabbath. From these sources, it is known that the rabbis concluded that there are 39 different types of work (Mishnah, sabbath 7.2). While some categories are very obvious, some are not. For example, a tailor who walks outside with a sewing needle attached to his garments would be guilty of violating the sabbath, since he was carrying his tools of work with him, thus carrying a burden. While the rabbis allowed for one to provide emergency medical treatment for someone who was in danger of dying, they would not allow that same person to render treatment to someone with an injury or illness which was not life-threatening (Misnah, sabbath 22.6).

Plucking grain on the sabbath (Matthew 12:1-8, Mark 2:23-28, Luke 6:1-5)

The synoptics narrate that Jesus and the disciples were traveling through the grain fields on a sabbath. Since they were hungry, the disciples decided to pluck some of the heads of grain in order to eat them. The Mosaic Law allowed for travelers to pluck some of the roadside grain when they were hungry (Deuteronomy 23:25). The Pharisees criticized Jesus and his disciples not because they plucked grain but because they did it on the sabbath. The gospels' presentation of Jesus' defense includes the following:

1. Jesus referred to the Old Testament story where David and his men technically broke the law when they ate the Holy Bread, which the Law reserved only for the priests. Now if Jesus and his disciples were wrong, so were David and his men, but they were not condemned by anyone for eating the bread. For Jesus, human need took precedence over the technicalities of the Law.
2. Mark includes Jesus saying: "The sabbath was made for humankind and not humankind for the sabbath." This means that divine law was made for human welfare, and humankind was not made to be a slave to a code of law.
3. Jesus apparently claimed to have the authority to reinterpret the sabbath Law when he said, "The Son of Man is Lord of the sabbath." The Law is not God; rather, God is over Law.
4. Due to Matthew's interest in the Law of Moses, Matthew would be particularly interested in how Jesus understood the sabbath law. Matthew presents these additional arguments:
   a. According to Matthew, Jesus encouraged his critics to learn the meaning of God's desire for mercy. Instead of an attitude of condemnation, Jesus encouraged them to exercise compassion toward others. For Jesus, mercy is more important than religious ritual. The priests technically break the sabbath by fulfilling their priestly duties.
   b. Priests offer sacrifices on the sabbath; they even perform circumcision in the 8th day if the 8th day falls on a sabbath.
   c. In contrast to these temple duties, something or someone is greater than the temple.

All these additional arguments show Matthew's great respect for the Law of Moses and the need to cultivate the proper attitudes. Without the proper attitude, the law is ineffective.

Healing on the sabbath (Matthew 12:9-14, Mark 3:1-6, Luke 6:6-11)

The text records that on a different occasion Jesus went to the synagogue on the sabbath and was involved in teaching. There was a man who had a withered hand. The synagogue elders watched closely to see if Jesus would violate the sabbath. Aware of the situation, Jesus told the man to stand and come to him. Then he asked, "Is it better to do good or harm on the sabbath?" He went on to point out that people will make efforts to save an animal in danger on the sabbath. If that is how people treat animals, what about human beings? Are not human beings of more value than all the animals? After he had made his case for merciful treatment of people on the sabbath, Jesus then healed the man.

It is important to notice that Jesus does not show disrespect for the Law of Moses nor the sabbath law. He supremely respected both the Law as a whole and the sabbath in particular. What Jesus objected to was the canonization of all the later traditions attached to the Law. Traditional interpretations are helpful guides to understanding God's will, but a helpful guide is not the same as a divinely inspired law. Jesus was particularly opposed to an enforcement of traditions which negatively affect people's lives. However, a certain group of religious leaders apparently believed that he was, in effect, rejecting the law. At the very least, he claimed to have authority to reinterpret and apply the law. This made Jesus dangerous, so a group of religious leaders began plotting to destroy him.

Controversy over exorcism--the source of Jesus' power (Matthew 12:22-37, Mark 3:19b-30, Luke 11:14-23,12:10)

Introduction

The controversy concerning the source of Jesus' power to drive out evil spirits appears to have been preserved separately from the other controversy stories. However, because of its similar theme of controversy, it will be discussed here.

Matthew, who connects this event with the healing of the man with the withered hand, states that Jesus withdrew to another area because of the dangers to his life. Mark only mentions that Jesus and the disciples left the area and went to the sea of Galilee. Immediately before this episode, Matthew summarizes Jesus' work in the Galilean area in order to show him as the fulfillment of the prophecy of Isaiah 42:1-4. In his preaching and healings, Jesus demonstrated himself to be the faithful servant of the Lord, who brings justice and compassion even to the Gentiles. Even Jesus' attitude and actions on the sabbath show him to be this compassionate servant-messiah. On the other hand, Mark as well as Luke emphasized that Jesus, after departing to Galilee, went up on a mountain for the purpose of selecting his twelve apostles.

The Controversy and Jesus' Response

According to Matthew, Jesus healed a blind and mute demoniac. The crowd was amazed and wondered if he might be the Son of David (i.e., Messiah). To counter this speculation, the Pharisees accused Jesus of performing exorcisms by the power of the devil (Beelzebub, prince of demons). Mark notes the controversy Jesus' ministry is causing but seems particularly interested in the negative attitudes of some of Jesus' family members. Jesus' response to the charge of being a servant of Beelzebub is that good never comes from the devil. Satan would not do anything to weaken his power. Jesus pointed out that it is a general truth that division from within leads to disaster. If Jesus was casting out by Satan's power, then Satan was in effect destroying himself; therefore, Jesus' power could not be from Satan.

Jesus also pointed out that some of the Pharisees' own disciples had been practicing exorcism. Where did they get their power? Then Jesus told a story about a burglar who broke into a strong man's house and stole his possessions. In this story, Jesus is a burglar who broke into the house of the strong man, Satan. Before robbing him, this burglar tied the strong man. Similarly Jesus will, or has, bound up Satan, and thus has been able to rescue people from the power of Satan. If Jesus' power is of the Holy

Spirit, it means that the kingdom of God has arrived and that one day Satan will be defeated and God will be reigning.

Jesus then warned the crowd about blasphemy of the Holy Spirit. He did not accuse anyone of this sin. Jesus probably hinted that the Pharisees could become guilty of this sin if they had not change. It is one thing to slander Jesus the man; it is quite another to slander God. They had attributed to the devil what actually came from God. The unintended implication of the Pharisees' theology is that evil comes from God—an inconceivable idea. When a person comes to a point that he regards God and Jesus as evil, that person will never be able to come to faith in Jesus as his savior, so blaspheming the Holy Spirit must be seen as a deliberate thought or action resulting from a hardened heart. This is the unforgivable sin. Jesus reminded his audience that it was well-known that the quality of the tree will naturally determine the quality of its fruit. The same is true with people. Jesus pointed out that the words of his critics reflected the evil in their character. The words of a person are the result of the character of that person. Since this is true, one should be aware that a person's words will be judged. We can be saved or condemned by our words. Careless, idle words are dangerous, as is carelessly expressing inappropriate thoughts and feelings. So then, Jesus used their own criticism of him as evidence of their own need for repentance and spiritual renewal.

Chapter 8

The Sermon on the Mount (Matthew 5-7 and Luke 6:20-49), Part 1

Introduction

Perhaps no body of teaching has had more influence on shaping Christian living than the Sermon on the Mount. There are two versions of this sermon; one is in Matthew and the other is in Luke. While there are many similarities between these accounts, there are also several differences.

1. Matthew states that Jesus gave this sermon from a mountain, while Luke says that Jesus taught from a level place. However, Luke noted earlier that Jesus went up to a mountain to pray and then came down to the level place.
2. Matthew's version is much longer than Luke's. Yet, nearly everything found in Matthew's version is in Luke, but scattered throughout the gospel instead of grouped together in a block.

How does one account for this discrepancy? One possible explanation is that Jesus' sermons and teaching may have been repeated. This is certainly possible, if not probable. But this theory does not explain everything. A second explanation is that Matthew's heavy emphasis on the teaching ministry of Jesus may suggest that he grouped several teachings of Jesus into a block, irrespective of when in Jesus' life they were said. In fact, scholars have noted that in Matthew there are five major blocks of teaching material:

Matthew 5-7. The Sermon on the Mount
Matthew 10. The Limited Commission of the Apostles
Matthew 13. Parables of the Kingdom
Matthew 18. Life in the Community of the Kingdom of God
Matthew (23)24-25. Divine Judgment and the End

Thus, for Matthew, preserving the teachings of Jesus was more important than preserving the exact chronology of Jesus' life. Most scholars believe the second explanation is correct. If so, then it means that the Sermon on the Mount in Matthew 5-7 faithfully represents the teachings of Jesus but that Jesus may not have given this sermon at any one time. Matthew 5-7 would be regarded more like an anthology of Jesus' teachings or a hypothetical sermon based on real teachings of Jesus.

This study will examine Matthew's version of the Sermon. Before engaging in this study, an outline of the sermon might be helpful.

Basic Outline of the Sermon according to Matthew

Theme: The Higher Righteousness of the Kingdom

1. Characteristics and mission of the ideal disciple. 5:3-16
    a. Beatitudes
    b. Salt and light
    c. Call to righteousness
2. The Ethic of Jesus in the Law of Moses. 5:17-48
    a. Murder
    b. Adultery
    c. Divorce
    d. Taking an oath
    e. Revenge
    f. Loving one's neighbors
3. Instructions concerning acts of worship and mercy. 6:1-18
    a. Giving alms

   b. Praying
   c. Fasting
4. Trust in God rather than in the world. 6:19-34
5. Exhortations about general conduct towards others. 7:1-12
6. Call to follow Jesus' teachings. 7:13-27

The Characteristics of the Ideal Disciple (Matthew 5:3-16)

The Beatitudes. 5:3-12

The sermon opens with a series of blessings upon persons who have certain qualities. Commonly known as the Beatitudes, this section of the sermon is designed to set the tone for the rest of the discourse. The key word is "Blessed," which can also mean "Happy" or "Oh, the Happiness!" The idea behind this word is a contentment in life or joy that is not dependent on one's personal circumstances. The Beatitudes are very structured—verses 3 and 10 contain the same blessing, "for theirs is the kingdom of heaven." On the surface, it appears that Jesus had in mind the present benefits of being a disciple, yet, verses 4-9 all place the blessing as something to be experienced in the undetermined future. This seems to indicate that those who develop the qualities mentioned in this teaching will receive their reward in the future, when the kingdom has been completely established. We can find happiness in the present, though, because we are encouraged that one day all the wrongs will be righted.

The first four beatitudes are concerned with the inner qualities required to be a disciple of Jesus.

First Beatitude - "Blessed are the poor in spirit". The phrase "poor in spirit" should be more accurately interpreted as spiritually poor. This is the awareness of one's spiritual needs. The first step in becoming a disciple of Christ is to be fully aware of one's need for God and all that he provides.

Second Beatitude - "Blessed are those that mourn". This may refer to God's comforting presence for all who are in grief. However, the word "mourn" was sometimes used to refer to sorrow over the fact that sin and death have such power in the world, and that everyone is vulnerable to sin. One might rephrase this to read, "Blessed is the person who is sensitive to evil, especially the evil in his life. This godly sorrow receives comfort in divine forgiveness."

Third Beatitude - "Blessed are the meek". The word translated "meek" is very similar to humility. Sometimes the word is translated as "gentleness." The Greeks often used this word to refer to the training of horses. This meaning implies that meekness is strength under control, or are the qualities of a disciplined person.

Fourth Beatitude - "Blessed are those who hunger and thirst for righteousness". The word-"righteousness" may mean either to be right with God or rightness of living. "Righteousness" may also be translated as "justice." Whether it refers to a relationship with God, one's moral character and life, or a more just-society, the key is that one yearns for this as a starving person hungers for food. One or all of these become the top priority of life.

The next three deal with the disciple's life in the world.

Fifth Beatitude - "Blessed are the merciful". This beatitude points out that disciples are to show kindness to others. Sometimes mercy refers to helping those who are undeserving.

Sixth Beatitude - "Blessed are the pure in heart". This kind of person is one whose heart is free of evil desires. Often the word "pure" refers to a singleness of heart, a heart with no ulterior motives. Such a person does good simply because he or she wants to do the right thing and please God. Thus, purity of heart is often reflected in one's conduct.

Seventh Beatitude - "Blessed are the peacemakers". This person is a reconciler, one who is able to brings conflict to an end and divided people together. Some have also suggested that the peace mentioned here is really peace with God and, therefore, peace of mind. But can there be peace with God and with oneself if there is not peace with one's neighbor? So it seems best to interpret Jesus' teaching to refer to all types of peacemaking, since the emphasis is on human relationships.

The final two beatitudes focus on the probability of experiencing persecution.

Eighth Beatitude - "Blessed are those who are persecuted for righteousness' sake".

Ninth Beatitude - "Blessed are you when people revile you and persecute you and utter all kinds of evil against you falsely on my account". These beatitudes are concerned with the disciples' life in a world which hates, slanders, and persecutes them. Jesus noted that this persecution took many forms: (1) "when people revile you"--demeaning words; (2) "and persecute you" --perhaps experiencing physical violence; (3) "and utter all kinds of evil against you falsely on my account" --slander. Jesus reminded the disciples that they need to understand that persecution has always been the lot of God's people. A true disciple must be willing to stand for his/her beliefs, no matter what the personal cost.

The Disciples are Salt and Light (Matthew 5:13-16, Luke 11:33;14:34-35)

As a means of emphasizing the importance of being one of his disciples and a citizen of the kingdom of God, Jesus compared the disciples to salt and light. Both salt and light are elements which have positive effects on life: one preserves and the other illuminates. Both are items which the world and each individual desperately need in order to live and grow. The point is that disciples are to make a difference in the world—to be an influence for good. Jesus concluded this illustration by pointing out that disciples of the kingdom are to be about doing good in the world, and by so doing, the world comes to recognize and give glory to God. Thus being a follower of Jesus means being a person whose life and work blesses others and leads them to praise God.

The Ethic of Jesus in the Law of Moses (Matt. 5:17-48)

Jesus and the Law (Matthew 5:17-20)

Most critics agree that Matthew was written with Jews or Jewish Christians in mind. One reason for this interpretation is that Matthew has included more material concerning the Law of Moses than the rest of the gospels. The issue which seems to have given cause for the section of the Jewish law concerns Jesus' attitude toward the Law. The sayings that Matthew has recorded argue that Jesus was never opposed to the Law of Moses, nor did he consider it to be unimportant and optional for God's people. However, he did oppose the religious traditions which had clouded the true nature and meaning of the law. Part of his ministry was to show the true meaning of the law.

Matthew 5:17-20 serves as an introduction to 5:21-48. In this section, Jesus stressed that he came to fulfill the Law and not destroy or abolish it. This seems to mean that as long as this earth stands the Law will have an ongoing validity. Furthermore, Jesus stated that the one who does not seek to keep the whole law, nor encourages others to, will be considered least in the kingdom. Only the one who has kept the entire law is considered great in the kingdom. Then Jesus concluded with this statement: "unless your righteousness exceeds that of the scribes and Pharisees, you will never enter the kingdom of heaven." This statement by Jesus has been described as the theme verse of Matthew's version of the Sermon on the Mount. Since the Pharisees were very meticulous concerning the minute regulations of the Law, how could disciples have a righteousness which exceeds that of the religious leaders? The answer is found in Jesus' emphasis on the inner qualities of discipleship. The outward is important, but the state of the heart is critical for following Jesus. This is the higher righteousness of the kingdom.

Jesus' Authoritative Interpretation of the Law (Matthew 5:21-48)

Introduction

Jesus had said that he came not to abolish the Law but to fulfill it. But what did he mean by fulfilling the Law? Since the Law itself is not prophetic, it is unlikely he meant some kind of historical fulfillment of some prediction. A better answer would point out that the law served out its purpose with the coming of Jesus. Or, as Paul put it, "the law was our disciplinarian until Christ came" (Galatians 3:24). However, the next section in the sermon in which Jesus commented on certain commands in the Law seems to require another interpretation of Jesus' fulfillment of the Law. In each of these comments on the Law, Jesus continually pointed to the inner quality of one's heart. In other words, commands which have to do with outward behavior, such as murder, is really about anger and hostility, the primary causes of murder. Thus in a real sense, Jesus fulfilled the law by revealing the true objective of the commandment.

Jesus' interpretation of the sixth commandment

"You have heard that it was said to those of ancient times, 'You shall not murder'; and 'whoever murders shall be liable to judgment.' But I say to you that if you are angry with a brother or sister, you will be liable to judgment" (Mathew 5:21-26).

Notice that Jesus often said, "You have heard that it was said ...But I say to you ...." This was to stress his authority to reinterpret and apply the Law of God. Jesus observed that the sixth commandment was really much more than a prohibition against murder. Rather, it was a prohibition against anything which could lead one to commit murder. In most cases, anger and hatred are attitudes which cause one to take another's life. Jesus pointed out that if anger is left unattended, it can grow into a type of attitude which is as evil as actual murder.

Beyond this, Jesus prohibited insults and demeaning references to another person. The English phrase "if you insult" literally means, "if anyone says to his brother 'stupid' or 'emptyheaded'" (from the Greek word, "raca"). Furthermore, the expression "fool" from the Greek "morei," is even more serious an insult. The word seems to be a stronger insult, referring to the spiritual or unspiritual condition of one's heart. This would be an extreme verbal put down, similar to the worst racist and sexist language today. Jesus anticipated a judgment in this life and in the life to come. Jesus also points out that it is necessary for a person to be reconciled with one's alienated brother or sister before one can even worship properly.

Jesus' interpretation of the seventh commandment

"You have heard that it was said, 'you shall not commit adultery.' But I say to you that everyone who looks at a woman with lust has already committed adultery with her in his heart" (Matthew 5:27-30).

Here Jesus seemed to argue that lustful desire is the same as the act of adultery, because the person wanted to do it and had thought about it. Jesus was not saying that physical or sexual attraction is wrong for unmarried people. Most people have those moments when a particular person of the opposite sex is very attractive to them. This is true because God made human beings with those hormones—it is very natural, but very different from lust. Lust is an obsessive desire for something or someone that is not permitted. Instead of trying to redirect the feelings to something positive, lust leads one to thoughts or actions that only increase desire, including the use of fantasy.

In order to prevent one from sinning, Jesus says that one should remove an eye or hand. Jesus was not commanding one to literally have one's hand amputated. Rather, Jesus meant that a person should be willing to do whatever it takes to be free from sin. Jesus warns against being thrown into "hell." The Greek word for "hell" is gehenna, which means the Valley of Hinnom. The Valley of Hinnom was a valley located outside the city of Jerusalem that was used in the first century as a garbage dump. In this place there were continually burning fires. It is easy to understand why this valley, with its perpetual fires, became the appropriate analogy for the place of eternal punishment.

Jesus' interpretation of the divorce law in Deuteronomy 24:1

"It was also said, 'Whoever divorces his wife, let him give her a certificate of divorce.' But I say to you that anyone who divorces his wife except on the ground of unchastity causes her to commit adultery; and whoever marries a divorced woman commits adultery" (Matthew 5:31-32).

In Jesus' day, only men had the right of divorce, and it was used with great frequency. Among the rabbis, there were two primary schools of thought concerning grounds for divorce. One was a fairly strict view, the other was very loose, and the latter view was the most popular. In this text, Jesus mentions unchastity as the only proper ground for divorce. The word "unchastity" is also translated "fornication" in other passages. The word means sexual immorality. Jesus said that unless unchastity is a husband's ground for divorce, then the divorce itself causes the woman to commit adultery. If she wasn't an adulteress before, the act of divorce will, in effect, make her into one. What does he mean by this?

He means that when a faithful woman is divorced she is, in effect, placed in an impossible situation. Women in the first century did not work outside the home. They were almost completely dependent on the support of some male, whether a father, family member, or husband. This meant that, in order to survive, a divorced woman must either marry or prostitute herself. In either case, she is with another man and thus an adulteress, according to the Law and tradition. The point of this instruction is that a husband should have more compassion on his wife, and not be so quick to divorce her. Divorce is a serious matter for all concerned, but for women, it has always been worse. Jesus is calling on husbands to begin thinking of someone other than themselves. Jesus' teaching here gave both protection and dignity to married women. He defined marital responsibility as a matter of compassion and unselfishness instead of a list of legal obligations.

Jesus' interpretation of the law concerning the making of a vow

"Again, you have heard that it was said to those of ancient times, 'you shall not swear falsely, but carry out the vows you have made to the Lord'" (Matthew 5:33-37).

According to the Mosaic Law, when one takes an oath or makes a vow, he or she is obligated to keep it. The taking of an oath usually involved some formalized ritual which might include offering a sacrifice to God. Jewish tradition had developed a complex system of taking oaths or making vows, a system that attached different levels of binding power for a vow or the truthfulness for an oath. This is similar to the modern-day expression " I swear on a stack of Bibles," as if that makes one's word more true.

For Jesus, the whole tradition was flawed because it ignored the basic fact that faithfulness and truthfulness are to be absolute qualities for a disciple of the kingdom. So, if a person promises that he or she will do something, it will be done. Or, if someone says something, people can trust that the statement is absolutely true. Disciples are to be people of honesty and integrity.

Jesus' interpretation of the law concerning retribution in Exodus 21:24

"You have heard that it was said, 'An eye for an eye and a tooth for a tooth'. But I say to you, do not resist an evildoer. But if anyone strikes you on the right cheek, turn the other also." (Matthew 5:38-42)

The Mosaic Law of an eye for an eye has to do with social justice, in which the punishment for any particular crime must be fitting for the crime. Therefore, the punishment for assault would be less severe than the punishment for premeditated murder. By the time of Jesus, however, the law was viewed as an endorsement for personal revenge. Under this system, the principle could be described as, "Do unto others what they have done to you." In contrast, Jesus taught that life in God's kingdom does not practice or endorse revenge. Instead of revenge, disciples should be extending forgiveness and love to all. Some have pointed out that Jesus never explained what one should do in some emergency situation, such as if a burglar tried to harm or kill a loved one. Nevertheless, the general principle of Jesus' words is that revenge and retaliation should not be part of the lifestyle of a follower of Jesus.

Jesus' interpretation on the Law concerning neighborly love in Leviticus 19:18

"You have heard that it was said, 'You shall love your neighbor and hate your enemy.' But I say to you, Love your enemies and pray for those who persecute you." (Matthew 5:43-48)

The Mosaic Law commanded the Israelites to love one another. In fact, the law even commanded that one should love the stranger or foreigner who was in their midst. Apparently, later tradition added the part about hating one's enemies. Conventional wisdom encouraged love for fellow Israelites but not necessarily anyone else. Jesus directly attacked the bigoted attitudes of many of his contemporaries. For Jesus, one's love should extend to all people, whether Jew or Gentile. This emphasis on compassion to the enemy shows that the love which is to be practiced in God's kingdom, must be love for all, including the unlovable and the undeserving. If God showers his blessing on everyone, irrespective of race, should not his children do the same? Perhaps this is what it means to be perfect as God is perfect.

Instructions Concerning Acts of Worship and Compassion (Matthew 6:1-18)

"Beware of practicing your piety before others in order to be seen by them; for then you have no reward from your Father in heaven." (Matthew 6:1)

This verse serves as an introduction to these instructions. The principal lesson is that the most important ingredient in acts of worship and compassion is the humility and unselfishness which should accompany everything that one does. Anyone who does these acts to be seen and praised by others receives only that reward. In fact, one might ask what the person's motivation was for doing these good deeds in the first place. Unfortunately, the person who seeks the approval of others is essentially doing these good works for selfish reasons. On the other hand, the one who desires only the approval of God will do these acts of piety out of love and respect for God. So again, Jesus pointed to the importance of the heart above the external act. Having laid a foundation for the practice of piety, Jesus then turned to specific religious acts.

Instructions concerning giving alms (Matthew 6:2-4)

In this section, Jesus stressed the need to give almost in secret. Whenever anyone tries to promote any good deed he or she is planning to do, he or she is guilty of self-righteous behavior. Jesus may have been referring to the conduct of some of the high officials who would give alms to the people in order to win the support of the average person. The danger is that when people leave God out of the picture and focus only on what they have done they behave as if they are more important than God.

Instructions concerning prayer (Matthew 6:5-8)

Jesus wanted his disciples not to be like the hypocrites who prayed publicly in order to receive praise from people. Prayer is supposed to be a time of private communion between the believer and God. Attempts to win over human opinion by how one prays is completely irrelevant and inappropriate. Jesus also stated that one should focus more on the content of one's prayer and the relationships that prayer can foster, rather than the citation of some pious phrase. God desires that prayers come from the heart of sincere believers.

The example of prayer in the Lord's prayer (Matthew 6:9-15).

Introduction to the prayer

This prayer should more properly be called the Model Prayer. The prayer does not contain everything that might be in a given prayer. For example, there is nothing about petitions for the sick, or expressions of thanksgiving for specific blessings experienced. Nevertheless, this prayer does contain the essentials that should be in every prayer. There are three parts to the prayer: (1)The opening; (2) The three petitions regarding the sovereignty of God; (3) The three petitions regarding human needs. This prayer will be discussed based on this outline.

1. The opening of the prayer - "Our Father in heaven". This opening focuses on both the loving and supporting nature of God as father and also the majestic power and authority of a God in heaven.
2. The three petitions regarding the sovereignty of God - "Hallowed by your name. Your kingdom come, Your will be done, on earth

as it is in heaven". These lines were composed in a poetic style in which each line is a restatement or elaboration of the previous one.

a. "hallowed be your name" means "let your name be held in reverence" or "let your name be regarded as holy"
b. "your kingdom come" explains how and when it will be when God's name is hallowed
c. "your will be done" explains how and when the kingdom comes. The name of God is hallowed when his kingdom comes, and his kingdom comes when God's will is done. Thus the kingdom of God is present wherever his will is done. Jesus' view of the kingdom can be described as the Rule of God in action.
d. Furthermore, each petition may have a personal application. For the person praying, therefore, this petition is more than simply a prayer for God to do something, but also a prayer of commitment to work to help bring these ideas into reality.

3. Three further petitions - concentrating on human need
   a. "give us this day our daily bread" This is the prayer for God to help provide us the physical necessities of life on a day by day basis. Like Israel in the wilderness who could only collect enough manna for the day's need, so also disciples must learn to trust God to help us on a daily basis. One acknowledges one's dependence on God for one's physical needs.
   b. "and forgive us our debts as we forgive debtors". This request shows the awareness of one's need for forgiveness. One's sins can be removed, but on the condition that the forgiven person will freely forgive others. One's sins are called debts. As sinners, we owe God more than we can possibly repay. Therefore, when God forgives us, it is truly an act of mercy. Jesus wants his disciples to extend mercy to others.
   c. "and do not bring us to the time of trial, but rescue us from the evil one". This petition requests that God not abandon one in the midst of temptation or difficulty. Therefore, this prayer is a confession that he/she needs God to survive spiritually.

The traditional closing of the Lord's prayer ("For the kingdom, the power, and the glory are yours, now and forever, Amen") does not appear in this text because the oldest and best manuscript copies of the gospel of Matthew do not include these words. While these verses are usually considered a later addition, probably originally a scribal note, this scribe blessed future readers of this prayer with a lovely and theologically powerful closing praise to God.

Instructions concerning fasting

Jesus assumes that most of his hearers will fast. Some will fast twice a week according to the Pharisaic tradition. Certainly, Jesus did not forbid fasting but insisted that it be done in the proper manner and with the proper attitude. As he said before, nothing is to be done for show or to impress others. Rather, one should do only that which brings honor and glory to God.

Chapter 9

The Sermon on the Mount, Part 2

Trust in God Rather than in the World (Matthew 6: 19-34)

In this part of the sermon, there is a shift in thought from instructions concerning acts of piety to an exhortation to place one's complete faith in God. But the shift in thought may be more apparent than real. The key lesson concerning acts of piety is that these should honor and please God and not one's fellow human beings. In other words, Jesus stressed the purity of heart and mind in carrying out an outward act. In this next section, disciples are called to have their priorities right. In other words, one should place trust in God instead of in the things of this world. The concern still has to do with a heart and mind devoted to God.

Treasures in Heaven (6: 19-21)

This section begins with a series of loosely connected brief instructions very similar to the wisdom instruction found in the Old Testament book of Proverbs. In the first small section, Jesus encourages people to desire things which last: the treasures in heaven over treasures on earth. The section closes with a stinging observation that one's treasure is what one constantly thinks about and desires. How revealing it is to realize that one's true treasure is what one places in his or her heart. That indicates the level of value they give to anything.

Light and Darkness (6: 22-23)

Usually, darkness refers to sin and the refusal to see the truth. The illustration of the good or ill health of the eye reflects how one sees things and people; whether with prejudice, jealousy and hatred (darkness), or caring, respect and love (light). Some commentators believe that the darkness refers to selfishness. If that is true, then to selfishly pursue only earthly treasures is to be in darkness.

God or Mammon (Material Things) (6: 24)

True discipleship places all things under God's rule. Jesus never said that wealth is evil in itself, but that it can become a tool for evil if a person allows it to rule or control him. But one must choose to trust and serve God and not the things of the world, especially money. God desires complete trust and devotion. It is all or nothing.

Trust God and Do Not Worry (6:25-34)

Different from the previous very short proverb-like statements, this is a much longer section, an almost poetic text on trust in God. Jesus used examples from nature to illustrate the goodness and care of God. God adorns nature more beautifully than all the wealth of Solomon. The point is that if God does this much for nature, one can be sure he will do this and even more for his people, for they are of more value than flowers or birds. The responsibility of the disciple is to set the right priorities in life: to seek God's kingdom first, which means to seek to do his will. Disciples should learn how to live one day at a time. The point is not that planning is wrong, but that one should live with the constant awareness that all one really has is today, and that one should trust in God for strength for that day. When the next day comes, then we can be concerned about it.

Conduct to others (Matthew 7:1-12)

This part of the sermon consists of another series of brief instructions connected generally around the general theme of proper conduct as disciples of Jesus.

Jesus forbids judging others (7:1-5)

The first exhortation has to do with self righteous attitudes. Jesus' words do not forbid the making of judgments of behavior based on God's law. Rather, Jesus was opposed to judgmental, critical attitudes toward others. Jesus warned that one's standard of judgment of others will be used on themselves. The parable of the log and speck stresses the folly of seeing the error in others while ignoring the wrong in oneself.

Pearls Before Swine (7:6)

While it is unclear why this saying is in the sermon, the main idea of the saying seems to be that one should not waste one's time sharing the message of the kingdom with those who show absolutely no interest. It is not necessary to condemn the nonbeliever; rather, it is wise to use one's energy and talents where it can do the most good, and leave the others in God's hands.

Additional teaching on Prayer (7: 7-11)

In a simple yet powerful way, Jesus exhorted believers to 'ask, seek, and knock' with the promise that God will hear and respond to his people. God will bless each person like a father blesses his son or daughter with good things. At first reading, it appears that Jesus promised that God would grant his people whatever they ask. Yet one must keep in mind that Jesus called on his disciples to seek treasures in heaven instead of treasures on earth, i.e., spiritual riches instead of material riches. In Luke's account of this saying, Jesus said that God will give the Holy Spirit to whomever asks—again an emphasis on spiritual blessings.

The Golden Rule (7:12)

This widely known and often repeated proverb appears in a slightly different form in the teachings of other wise persons:

1. Rabbi Hillel: What is hateful to yourself, do to no other.
2. Book of Tobit (4:6): What you yourself hate to no man do.
3. Confucius: What you do not want done to yourself, do not do to others.
4. The Greek King Nicocles: Do not do to others the things which make you angry when you experience them at the hands of other people.
5. Stoic proverb: What you do not wish to be done to you, do not to anyone else.

While the content of all these sayings is very similar to Jesus' sayings, there is one basic difference. Jesus stressed what one must do, instead what one must not do. The implied lesson of other "golden rules," is that one must avoid behavior that is hurtful in some way to others (i.e., lie, steal, cheat, injure, kill, etc.). Such a principle of life can be fulfilled by doing nothing at all. But the positive version of Jesus' teaching compels one to action and involvement in the lives of others. If we want to be respected, then we must show respect. And if we want to be loved and cared for, then we must love and care for others. The lesson of the Golden Rule is that concern for others becomes the watchword of moral living for a citizen of God's kingdom.

Call To Follow His Teachings (Matthew 7:13-27)

The sermon comes to an end with a charge and an invitation. If we desire to be in the Kingdom of God, we must conform our lives to the will of

God. But the will of God is not simply an exercise in rule keeping. Others have kept the Law but never found the kingdom. Sometimes a focus on meticulous rule keeping leads to an attitude of arrogance and self-righteousness. Other times it results in seeking the minimum requirements for salvation. With both attitudes the focus, the faith, and the commitment is not on God, but oneself. The Sermon calls people to place their entire trust in God and allow him to lead them in the direction he chooses. Such is not easy and takes great endurance and courage to maintain. This conclusion of the sermon is an invitation to make the hard choice to trust in God and follow his will in every area of life.

The Narrow and Wide Gate (7:13-14)

The text begins with a description of discipleship which is hard and long, but a rewarding journey. The crowd normally goes the easy and wide way, which is ultimately destructive. Following Jesus is described as entering through a narrow gate and traveling on a hard (steep and curvy) road. Unfortunately Jesus said only a few will have the wisdom and courage to take the hard road. But those who do will experience a quality of life unknown by most people.

A Warning Against False Prophets (7:15-23)

Jesus warned his disciples concerning the dangers of false prophets. To the unsuspecting person, these prophets will appear harmless and sincere, but this is all a deception. The genuineness of a prophet can be detected by people, if they look for the right things. They are to look for a prophet's "fruits," which means his or her conduct and words; do they lead one closer to or away from God? Just because someone knows the right religious words to say, such as "Lord, Lord," and can even do marvelous deeds associated with the work of a prophets (to prophesy and cast out demons in the Lord's name), a true prophet, as well as a true disciple, is one who does the will of God. Jesus' words serve not only as a warning to any self-proclaimed prophet, but for anyone who claims to be one of his disciples.

Call to obedience (7:24-27)

The sermon concludes with the familiar parable of the two builders. The parable is designed to remind people that knowing and believing the word of God is not enough to be a faithful disciple in the world. This knowledge and faith must be put into practice in a submission to the will of God, which is seen in one's conduct and daily life decisions.

In the parable of the two builders, the house could represent one's life. The foundation upon which the house was built would be the foundation upon which one builds his or her life. This latter foundation would include a person's philosophy of life, ethics, and sense of values. A foundation of sand is a foundation of the values of the world, which are primarily material, temporary, and rooted in selfishness. In contrast, the foundation of rock is a foundation on the teachings of Christ, which he says has permanent significance. The storm would represent some crisis in life that would test the foundation of a person's life. For the early church it might have been poverty or persecution or war. Jesus says that the person whose life is founded on God's word as reflected in his teachings will survive the crisis and go on to live a victorious life, a life according to the higher righteousness of the Kingdom of God.

Chapter 10

The Parables of the Kingdom (Matthew 13)

Introduction

After the controversy concerning the source of Jesus' power to perform exorcism, in which he said that a house divided against itself cannot stand (Mark 3:20-27), Mark states that Jesus warned the people against blaspheming the Holy Spirit (3:28-30), and responded to those who spoke of his family that his real family are those who do the will of God (3:31-35). Then in chapter 4, Mark presents several parables of Jesus. Matthew and Luke also record these same parables in approximately the same historical context as Mark, sometime after the Sermon on the Mount. Continuing the interest in Jesus as a teacher, these parables will be discussed here.

Definition of a parable

Literally the Greek word for "parable" comes from two Greek words which together mean, "thrown alongside," some thing or idea is placed by the side of another thing or idea for comparison or analogy. Jesus often told stories from real-life human experiences, or briefly referred to something from real life in order to teach some important spiritual lesson. Thus the old definition of a parable has real truth in it: "an earthly story with a heavenly meaning." The gospels, however, used the word "parable" in a very loose way. Sometimes it meant a story, and other times a brief illustration. Often the stories portrayed life experiences which either could have happened or often did happen. Other times, Jesus told stories with a high degree of exaggeration in order to make his point. The power of a parable is in the central idea or lesson of the parable and not in the minute details found in the parable.

The gospels indicate that the parable was one of the most common teaching tools Jesus used. But why did Jesus speak in parables? According to Mark, Jesus explained that parables were a kind of teaching designed to separate/distinguish the believers from the unbelievers (4:10-12); believers understand the parables, while the unbelievers do not. Matthew gives the same reason, but with more explanation (13:10-23). For the believer and honest searcher, the parables reveal wonderful truths about the kingdom, while the closed-minded and unbeliever see only stories. Now some of the parables communicate a message which even the most closed-minded could understand, such as the Good Samaritan, or the prodigal son. While it is clear that Jesus did not invent the parable as a means of teaching, he is widely recognized as the one who mastered the art of parable.

Kingdom Parables

The parables to be examined in this section are commonly called the parables of the kingdom. Since the heart of Jesus' message was the Kingdom of God, one could argue that all the parables of Jesus are kingdom parables. But most of the parables in this section explicitly claim to be metaphors of some quality of the kingdom. One can perceive a particular quality of the kingdom by determining the main point of the parable.

The Parable of the Sower (Matthew 13:1-9, 18-23, Mark 4:1-9,13-20, Luke 8:4-8, 11-15)

While there is no specific mention of the kingdom in this parable, it clearly has all the other characteristics of a kingdom parable. This parable is about a farmer planting seed in anticipation of a good harvest. Like the farmers of the Middle East, both ancient and modern, the farmer does not carefully plant individual seeds in straight rows on clean and plowed soil. Instead, he takes seeds from his seed bag and throws the seed in every direction. Consequently, seed fell on a variety of soils, from which came a variety of results.

"Some seed fell on the path"

Paths in Palestinian fields were the common paths that travelers would use on their journeys. The ground in the pathway was usually hardened by the pounding of feet, making it virtually impossible for the seed to penetrate the soil and, as the story indicates, the birds ate up the exposed seed.

"Some seed fell on rocky ground"

Rocky ground does not refer to soil mixed with stones, like gravel, but to a thin layer of earth under which lay a shelf of rock. There may be only a few inches of soil over the shelf of rock, and, as the parable says, there was not sufficient depth of soil to help produce a strong plant. Consequently, the plant died under the hot sun.

"Other seed fell among thorns"

It is not clear exactly what this soil may have looked like. It may have been a typical weed patch, which may be found on the sides of the road or farm field. However, this thorny ground may have looked initially like weeded soil, until the plants started to grow. If this were the scenario assumed in this parable, then it was certain that the seed would not produce a strong crop, for weeds grow at a speed and strength which can threaten even healthy plants. In this case, the weeds choked the life out of the good plant until it died.

"Other seed fell into the good soil"

This is soil which is clean, deep, and soft--soil which had been prepared for planting. The presence of nutrients help plants grow more easily and thus produce a good harvest.

Interpretation of the parable

This parable is one of only two parables where Jesus interprets the meaning of the various elements. For example, the soil on the path represents those who hear the word but do not understand it. The failure to understand probably means the refusal to understand, i.e., hardness of heart. When someone refuses to listen and understand the gospel, the devil will eventually remove that opportunity from the person.

Secondly, the rocky soil represents those people who accept the gospel enthusiastically but only superficially. With no root and no depth of faith, it is inevitable that with the first sign of trouble such a person would fall, since there was never any genuine faith or commitment.

Thirdly, the thorny ground is symbolic of the cares of the world which can choke a new faith. Without a thorough weeding through repentance and obedience, the old ways of worldliness can kill the spiritual life.

Finally, the seeds on good soil represent someone who hears and accepts the gospel with a pure and honest heart. Such a person will bear fruit, perhaps in significant changes in one's personal life.

While Jesus' explanations of the various soils may lead one to believe that the parable was originally addressed to the crowd, exhorting them to be careful how they hear God's word, the original intent of the parable was to encourage the disciples and others to continue in faithfulness in the spreading of the gospel. Jesus called this parable the parable of the sower. So the emphasis is on the sower, the preacher who devotes his energies to spreading the message of the kingdom of God. This parable assures the reader that despite all the disappointments in ministry, ultimately the kingdom will grow because some will believe.

The Parable of the Wheat and Weeds (Matthew 13:24-43)

Only the gospel of Matthew records this parable, and it is the second of the two parables that Jesus explained to his disciples. The emphasis on divine judgment and threats from within the kingdom are more in line with what was of particular concern to Matthew.

Background to the parable of the wheat and weeds

Weeds have always been a problem for farmers. The weeds described in this parable are a type of weed, called darnells or tares. In the early stages of growth it is impossible for one to distinguish between the weed and the wheat. Later, as the plant matures, the weed can so intertwine itself around the wheat that one cannot pull the weed out without pulling some of the wheat. Thus, the only realistic opportunity for one to separate the wheat from the weeds is during harvest. Separating the weed from the wheat is important because the weed is slightly poisonous. The weeds can be separated only by hand. The grain is spread out over a large tray and then the harvester picks the wheat out from the weeds. Jesus told a parable in which one farmer, seeking to sabotage a neighboring farmer's crop, secretly has tares sown into the neighbor's field. When the farmer discovers this, he declares that weeding will have to wait until the harvest in order to save the wheat.

Interpretation of the parable

Based on this background information, it may be an interpretation of the parable may be suggested. Like a farmer who has servants that plant a farm field, Jesus sent his disciples into the world to preach and make disciples. Yet, the devil, Jesus' enemy, is also planting evil in God's kingdom by planting evil people within it in order to destroy the kingdom. When both the good and evil develop to the point that they are not easily distinguishable, one must wait until the harvest or judgment day for separation to occur. The lesson of the parable is good and evil must and will co-exist until the judgment. Judgment and separation is finally a divine work. When people attempt to cast out all suspected heretics and sinners from the church, the kingdom can suffer terribly. While it is right to have concern for false brethren, this parable teaches that disciples are not to carry on premature judgments. There will inevitably be a day of reckoning for all.

Parables of the Mustard Seed and the Leaven (Matthew 13:31-33, Mark 4:30-32, Luke 13:18-19)

Introduction

These are parables concerning the growth of the kingdom. The fact that there are two similar parables coupled together suggest that these two parables were probably originally preserved together, perhaps even during the oral stage of gospel tradition. These parables both speak of confidence and optimism concerning the future of the Kingdom of God. In both parables, something small ultimately experiences significant growth.

The Mustard Seed

The mustard seed is a common symbol for smallness in the Middle East. The mustard seed can grow into a treelike plant averaging 7 to 8 feet tall and can sometimes reach heights of 12 to 15 feet. The point of the parable is that the kingdom starts from the smallest beginning, but will grow to unbelievable size. When Jesus told the parable, the following of Jesus was still small, so this was a prophecy of future growth and triumph of the Kingdom of God.

The Leaven or Yeast

Leaven is fermented dough saved from a previous batch in order to make the next batch. The point of the parable is also about the growth of the kingdom. However, the growth described in this parable is more of an expansion due to inner transformation, just as leaven or yeast in the dough causes the lump to expand and become something good to eat. Perhaps the inner transformation refers to the disciples/missionary or the transforming of men and women by the power of the gospel. Jesus may also have had in mind the transformation of a society through the influence of Christianity.

The Hidden Treasure and Pearl of Great Price (Matthew 13:44-46)

Only Matthew has preserved these two parables of discovery, one discovery by accident and one discovery after searching. In both stories, Jesus stated that when the treasure is found the discoverers both recognize the wealth of their find and joyfully sell all their possessions in order to have the treasure. As with the parables of the mustard seed and the leaven, most likely the parables of hidden treasure and pearl were preserved together in the early decades of the Church.

The Hidden Treasure

In the ancient world, the common practice was for people to bury their valuables in the ground. Similarly, soldiers would often bury their treasures before a battle. This parable gives no clues as to why the man was digging in the ground. He may have been looking for lost buried treasure or may have simply been digging in order to bury something of his own. Some have suggested that Jesus was describing a common day laborer who, while in the process of digging, accidentally finds a treasure. It is clear that he was not digging on his own land for later he purchases the land in order to have the treasure. The man's reason for digging is really irrelevant to this story. The importance of the story comes when the man finds the treasure and decides to sell everything he owns in order to have it. Why did the man sell everything he owned in order to have the field and thus the treasure? The story clearly implies that the treasure was worth more than all the man possessed. In other words, the man knew that by selling everything he had for the field and treasure, he was not losing anything but actually gaining. The point is that the kingdom of God is worth all that a person has. When one discovers the kingdom and understands what he or she has found, he or she is faced with a decision, "Shall I give up everything in order to have the kingdom or not?"

The Pearl of Great Price

The second parable is about a traveling merchant looking for pearls. He eventually finds one of exceptional value and beauty. Consequently, he sells his entire stock of pearls and the rest of his possessions in order to buy the one pearl. In this story, Jesus pictured someone who was on a search for something of great value. Not only was he in search of pearls, but the parable also suggests that this man was an expert on pearls. He knew what to look for in good pearls and could not be fooled by a counterfeit. Again, when he finally found the pearl he had been looking for, perhaps for most of his life, he was faced with the decision about whether or not he was willing to pay the price for the pearl. Without hesitation, he gave up everything because he had found something far more precious than all his possessions.

Jesus knew that many of his hearers were like this traveling merchant: they, too, were searching for something of great value. Instead of some precious jewel, they were searching for the kingdom of God, which is more than any earthly treasure. Note that the merchant, like the laborer in the field, willingly sold all that he had. Why? Because he knew that he was not losing anything, but, in fact, he was gaining everything. If this is true for earthly treasure, it is even more so for the kingdom of God.

The Dragnet (Matthew 13:47-50)

Introduction

Found only in Matthew, this is a parable concerning the makeup and judgment of the kingdom. Similar in theme to the parable of the wheat and the weeds, this parable also stresses the non-discriminatory spirit of the kingdom. Everyone is invited, and a wide diversity of people will respond.

Background to the Parable

There were two ways to fish in ancient Palestine. One was the casting method. Using this method, a person would throw a fishnet into the water from the shore. The fisherman first looks for fish in the shallow water on the shoreline, and then casts the net, which sinks to the bottom, trapping the fish. The other method of fishing was the dragnet method. The fisherman would use a square net with cords on each corner. When the boat moved across the water, the net would drag behind, collecting all kinds of fish in its cone shape.

The Message of the Parable

In this parable, a fisherman throws the net into the lake from the rear of the boat. As expected, the net caught all kinds of sea creatures. When the net was pulled ashore, the fisherman opened the net and separated the usable from the unusable fish. The unusable are thrown back into the water, but the usable are kept. In this everyday occurrence of the ancient Middle East, Jesus said that something about the Kingdom of God can be seen. Like that net, the kingdom is bound to be a mixture of all kinds of people. No one is denied because of nationality or social class. In fact, both good and evil people enter in. Some are sincere, while others are hypocritical. Some are useful, while others are useless. Finally, there will be a separation or judgment. This judgment is again described as a divine privilege. The bad fish probably are an analogy to the useless ones who could harm or have no commitment to the kingdom. These useless ones also have no commitment to the kingdom.

Treasures New and Old (Matthew 13:51-52)

Matthew concludes this part of his gospel with a parable-like illustration of someone who honors both old and new treasures, so Jesus' teaching brings together the best of the Old Law with his new ways.

Chapter 11

The Ministry of Jesus in Galilee and Beyond, Part 1

Four Miracles Which Demonstrate A Certain Aspect Of Jesus' Power

As noted before, the gospels often grouped stories and sayings of Jesus together. Sometimes the gospel writer may have received a group of stories or sayings as they had been preserved by early Christians. Other times the writers themselves may have created a group for theological purposes. Many scholars believe that the gospel of Mark grouped several stories together and that Matthew and Luke followed Mark's example. One place where this appears to have happened is in a series of miracle stories found in the same order in all three gospels. Mark apparently brought these four stories together in order to highlight a different aspect of Jesus' power:

1. Stilling the storm - power over nature
2. Exorcism - power over demons or demonic forces
3. Healing the women with the flow of blood - power over disease
4. Raising the daughter of Jairus - power over death

Taken together, the message of the four stories seems to be that Jesus' power extends over all of the created order, especially those arenas over which Satan and his servants ruled. In other words, the kingdom of God has arrived in the person and ministry of Jesus. If Jesus has power over everything, then he truly is the Son of God. The stories appear in different places in each gospel's narrative. Since Mark places them immediately following the parables of the kingdom, the stories will be discussed at this point.

Stilling the Storm (Matthew 8:18-27, Mark 4:35-41, Luke 8:22-25)

The Sea of Galilee is notorious for sudden storms. The word "storm" is a word that could mean earthquake, referring to the violent shaking a boat would experience because of rough waves. Note the contrast between Jesus and the disciples. Jesus was asleep while they were awake and terrified. As the storm increased in intensity, the disciples became more frightened. In desperation they awakened Jesus and complained to him about the crisis. In Mark, the disciples appear to be somewhat angry at Jesus for appearing to be disinterested in their problem. Matthew and Luke only mention that they were afraid. Jesus responded by calming the storm with a simple word of command, "Peace, be still." Then he rebuked the disciples for their lack of faith. Faith in what? Faith that God would protect them? Faith that if they asked God he would answer? Faith in Jesus and his power? The disciples responded with feelings of awe and wonder that Jesus could command even the wind and sea. Thus, this traveling teacher from Galilee demonstrated a power over nature similar to how God created and ordered the world: by his powerful word.

The Gerasene Demoniac (Matthew 8: 28-34, Mark 5:1-20, Luke 8:26-39)

Matthew's account mentions that there were two demoniacs, while Mark and Luke mention only one. According to Mark and Luke, this man lived among the tombs, among the caves of the dead. He could not be restrained or bound, even with chains, since his superhuman strength often broke the chains into pieces. Every day, no matter the time, the man would continually let out a shriek or cry—one of utter despair and anguish. Mark adds that the demoniac would bruise himself with stones, which may refer to some twisted form of demon worship or simply acts of masochism. At the sight of Jesus, the demon-possessed man instantly recognized him as the Son of the Most High God and bowed down before him.

The demoniac called himself Legion. This was not a real name, but rather a nickname or description of the man's current spiritual condition. The word "legion" was well-known in those times to be the name of the largest contingent of Roman soldiers, usually between 3000 and 5000 men. The fact that this man is called Legion signifies that this man is possessed by a multitude of demons. Thus Jesus is not simply facing a single demonic power, but a concentration of thousands of demons. The story points out that Jesus had complete control of these demons. They had to submit to his word of command. The text says that the demons begged Jesus to send them into a herd of swine. Jesus agreed and thus delivered the man of his demon possession. At the permission of Jesus, the demons went into a herd of swine, which ran over a cliff and perished. The townspeople reacted to this event with fear and asked Jesus to leave. As for the restored man, Jesus told him to go back to his family and friends and tell them what God had done for him.

Jairus' daughter and the woman with the hemorrhage (Matthew 9:18-26, Mark 5:21-43, Luke 8:40-56)

The final two stories are interrelated in some very interesting ways. One is the story of a little girl of 12 years of age who was very ill and a woman who had been ill for 12 years. The healing of the woman unintentionally contributed to the death of the little girl, which led Jesus to raise the girl back to life. Other than Jesus' resurrection, there are only three resurrection stories recorded in the gospels. The story of Jairus' daughter is the only one found in more than one gospel (it is found in all three synoptic gospels).

The story begins with the arrival of Jesus in a town, possibly Capernaum (Matthew 8:5, 9:1). Jairus asked Jesus to come and heal his daughter. All of the gospels point out that Jairus was the leader of the local synagogue, which probably means that he was a Pharisee and a rabbi. In response, Jesus agreed to go to his sick and dying daughter, but as Jesus was walking through the city to Jairus' house, a large crowd gathered around him and a woman touched the edge of his cloak.

This woman had had some kind of hemorrhage or flow of blood for 12 years. She had tried everything to be healed. Mark said that she "endured much under many physicians," a telling commentary on the state of the medical profession at that time. No matter what she tried she continued to be sick, so her problem was more than simply one of chronic illness. According to the Mosaic Law, her flow of blood had made her perpetually unclean for the twelve years of her disease. To be ceremonially unclean meant that she had been socially ostracized and banned from the synagogue. No one was to be near her or touch her or else they would also be unclean. Therefore, when the woman went up to Jesus and touched his garment, she was in violation of the ritual purity codes. Her act, though, was also a demonstration of bold and courageous faith in the power of Jesus. The result of her touch of faith was that her hemorrhage instantly stopped. Aware that healing power had gone out of him, Jesus stopped and inquired who it was that had touched him. When the woman came forward in fear and trembling, Jesus praised the woman for her faith, assured her of the healing, and sent her home with a blessing. Jesus had healed an incurable disease because of a woman's faith.

But this miracle had delayed Jesus' arrival at Jairus' house. When he finally arrived, the child was dead, yet Jesus stated that he could bring her to life again. He brought his three closest disciples, Peter, James and John, into the house. The people on the outside, who had been weeping in public lamentation for the death of the girl, laughed at Jesus for claiming he could awaken her. The miracle is described very simply. First, Jesus went alone into the room where the body of the child lay. Then he said "Talitha cumi" which means "Little girl, arise." Immediately, the girl woke up and arose, to the amazement of all.

The choosing and sending of the twelve (Matthew 10, Mark 3:13-19a, Luke 9:1-6; 10:1-16)

Introduction

Mark and Luke record that Jesus chose his twelve apostles early in his ministry (Mark 3:13-19a, Luke 6:12-16). However, Luke also has an account of the commissioning of the twelve apostles (9:1-6) and other disciples (10:1-16). Matthew only contains the commission of the twelve. Nothing specific is said about Jesus choosing twelve out of a larger number, only that he sent them on a specific mission. So while Mark only tells of the choosing of the twelve, with virtually nothing said about the work of the twelve, Matthew only tells of the mission of the twelve. Luke has both. Interestingly, the words of Jesus to the twelve in Matthew 10 are virtually the same as the instruction given to the seventy in Luke 10. Probably Matthew has pulled together, into one large discourse, the teachings of Jesus concerning the mission of a disciple of Jesus. It is well known that Jesus chose twelve apostles. The number twelve must have been chosen deliberately for its symbolic power. (The number twelve was symbolic of the twelve tribes of Israel.) As proclaimers of the imminent kingdom of God, these twelve probably signified the beginning of the New Israel, the True People of God.

The names and characters of the disciples

Simon, who is called Peter, and Andrew, the sons of John

Simon is usually portrayed in the gospel story as impulsive and unpredictable, yet, he is also seen as the natural leader of the twelve. The synoptic gospels say nothing about Andrew. However, the gospel of John described Andrew as the one who brought Simon and others to Jesus (John 1:40-41,6:8; 12:22).

James and John, the sons of Zebedee

The next two apostles are the Sons of Zebedee--James and John. Mark adds that Jesus nicknamed them "Boanerges," which means "Sons of Thunder." They may have been given this nickname because they were known for their violent tempers or tendency to fight.

Philip

Nothing is said of Philip in the synoptic gospels. In John, Philip is portrayed as the one who demands tangible proof concerning the claims of Jesus (14:8).

Bartholomew

Bartholomew, the sixth apostle, isn't portrayed by any of the gospels, although some scholars have speculated that the Nathaniel in the gospel of John is Bartholomew.

Thomas

The seventh apostle is Thomas. He is sometimes called "Didymus," which means "the twin." One explanation is that Thomas was considered to look so much like Jesus that he could have been mistaken as Jesus' twin brother. In John, Thomas is the one who would not believe in the resurrection unless he could see and touch the wounds of the risen Jesus (20:24-25).

Matthew the tax collector and James the son of Alphaeus

Matthew the tax collector is the eighth apostle in Matthew's list. In Mark and Luke, he is called Levi, indicating his priestly heritage. Mark 2:14 says that Levi (Matthew) was the son of Alphaeus, which may indicate that Matthew was the brother of James the son of Alphaeus the ninth apostle.

Thaddaeus

Apparently, Thaddaeus is the same as the Judas son of James in Luke 6:16.

Simon the Cananaean

Matthew and Mark call the next to last apostle Simon the Canaanaean; Luke calls Simon the Zealot. A zealot was a political revolutionary who believed that the kingdom of God would be established only by means of military force. They opposed the Roman occupation of Palestine and the imposition of taxes. In many respects, they were the descendants of the Maccabees who liberated the Jews from Syrian oppression. They were similar to many terrorists groups today. Either Simon believed Jesus would bring about the zealot's dream, or Simon had left the group in order to follow Jesus.

Judas Iscariot, who betrayed him (Matthew 10:2-4)

The twelfth and last apostle to be named is Judas Iscariot, the one who betrayed him. According to John, Judas was the treasurer of the group (12:6). The name "Iscariot" may mean that the Judas came from the village of Kerioth in Judea, or it may be a variation of the name "Scarrii," the knife men, the name for a group of terrorists.

The limited commission of the twelve (Matthew 10:5-42)

Introduction

Jesus' instructions to his apostles concerning their mission can be found in each of the synoptic gospels. However, where these instructions are somewhat scattered throughout the gospels of Mark and Luke, they are grouped together in Matthew. In fact, Matthew's version is the fullest set of instructions concerning the mission of the disciples. Though Matthew has the most verses on this topic, it does not follow that the record of Mark and Luke can be ignored. In each version an obvious difference in emphasis is employed. Mark has the briefest account and seems to stress the roles that sacrifice, faith, and suffering will have in the disciples' mission. Building on Mark, Luke mentions that the disciples were selected after Jesus had spent the entire night in prayer. The disciples' mission will be to proclaim the kingdom of God and to heal (Mark mentions only casting out evil spirits). In order to face the prospects of suffering and personal rejection, Luke includes passages that call for courage in the face of danger and commitment in the face of rejection. Matthew shares much of Mark's and Luke's emphasis, but adds that this mission was not a universal one but specifically to the lost sheep of the house of Israel. Furthermore, while Matthew also notes that the disciples are to preach concerning the kingdom, he stresses that the kingdom is at hand. There is a sense of urgency in Matthew's version because judgment is expected at any moment. Matthew's point is that Jesus first sent his disciples to the Jews in order to prepare for the coming of the kingdom of heaven. At the end of the gospel of Matthew, Jesus sends them to the whole world.

Analysis of Matthew 10:5-42

The essence of Jesus' limited commission of his disciples was to preach and to heal. Along with healing, they were given the power to cast out evil spirits. Jesus sent them to the Jews, or the lost sheep of the house of Israel. They were to go with minimum material possessions. Their preaching and healing was to be done freely. In each town, they were to seek out a reputable home to stay in and stay there as long as they stayed in that town, whether the host was friendly or not. If the town completely rejected their message, then they were to leave that home or town, and shake off their dust as a sign of judgment.

Jesus promised that the future would bring trials and hardships for the disciples. The disciples would be forced to answer for their faith and even for false charges against them. Nevertheless, the disciples must not be frightened, for the Holy Spirit would guide them in their responses to the authorities. The disciples should also expect to suffer persecution. Some would be rejected by their families. Persecution would cause the disciples to be objects of hatred. Others would be killed. Disciples should try to avoid persecution by moving from one hostile town to another, but, as horrible and frightening as persecution is, they should never forget that their suffering would be no more than the suffering of their master. It is because they follow him that they would be persecuted. If the messiah is to suffer, they should also expect to suffer.

In view of the persecution that he said would come, Jesus offered his disciples assurance from God. He exhorted them not to fear the persecutor, who could only hurt or kill a person's physical body. God is the one who controls a person's eternal destiny, so if one trusts and obeys, he or she will have little to fear. Moreover, Jesus promised that God would not forget any of his disciples. After all, human beings, especially followers of Jesus, are more important than the animals, and he cares deeply for them.

Therefore, Jesus encouraged the disciples never to fail to confess their faith, for there is reward and blessing for those who confess faith despite threats. Conversely, there is rejection and punishment for those who, out of fear, do not confess. Jesus further warned the disciples that preaching the gospel will sometimes cause unrest, even among families. Yet, each disciple must love Jesus more than his or her own family. The hard call of Jesus is that each disciple must give his or her highest commitment to Jesus.

Using the metaphor of the cross, Jesus called his followers to a life of extreme self-sacrifice. For the disciple of Jesus, true life is found in losing one's life or giving it up. It is like undergoing a spiritual death followed by a spiritual resurrection. True discipleship is complete submission to God's will.

Jesus then promised future blessing and rewards for those who accept this call to discipleship and live it out. Those who accept the call of Jesus and show hospitality to one of these specially commissioned messengers will be rewarded. The one who welcomes and serves a prophet or a righteous person will be given the same blessing and reward as the prophet or righteous person.

Chapter 12

The Ministry of Jesus in Galilee and Beyond, Part 2

A Review of John the Baptist's Death (Matthew 14:1-12, Mark 6:14-29, Luke 9:7-9)

After Jesus sent his disciples out on their mission, Mark and Luke mentioned that Herod Antipas had heard of the current ideas concerning Jesus and concluded that he was John the Baptist raised from the dead. The idea was particularly bothersome to Herod since he had been responsible for the beheading of John. Herod may have had a guilty conscience because of what happened to John. He may have concluded that John had come back to haunt him. Whatever the reason for Herod's behavior, Mark, followed closely by Matthew and Luke, used this situation to review what had happened to John. This story is told in retrospect, so it is difficult to know just when during Jesus' life the death of John took place.

The gospels recount that John the Baptist had condemned the unholy marriage of Herod to Herodias, the wife of Herod's brother Philip. Herodias apparently agreed to this marriage in order to become something like a queen. The historian Josephus reported that, in order to marry Herodias, Herod had to first divorce his first wife, a daughter of the

Arabian king Aretas. When the first wife received the news of the divorce, she fled home and told her father of the dishonor Herod had shown her. In angry response, Aretas waged war against Herod and defeated him, but was halted by the Romans who came to Herod's rescue.

After the marriage to Herodias, Herod had John arrested in order to quiet his criticism and please his new wife. According to Mark, Herod protected John from the murderous plans of his new wife Herodias. Moreover, Mark also indicates that Herod even listened to John voluntarily. He apparently respected John as a prophet and a man of integrity. Matthew further points out that even though Herod also wanted John dead, he feared the populace because they respected John as a prophet. This agrees with the testimony of Josephus, who stated that John's wide popularity may have been a deterrent to any harm immediately coming to him. Eventually, though, that protection was removed and John was killed (Antiquities 18.5.2).

Matthew and Mark both note that there was a party held in honor of King Herod's birthday. The daughter of Herodias (Josephus named her Salome) danced for Herod. Herod was so impressed with her dancing that in a drunken state he offered her anything, up to half of his kingdom. After receiving counsel from her mother, the daughter asked for the head of John the Baptist. While he was reluctant to do it, Herod fulfilled her request and ordered John's execution.

The feeding of the multitude (Matthew 14:13-21, Mark 6:30-44, Luke 9:10-17)

Introduction

The feeding of the 5000 is the only miracle performed by Jesus recorded in all four gospels (see also John 6:1-15). The synoptic gospels place this narrative immediately after the story of the death of John the Baptist. Matthew notes that after the burial of John the disciples went back to Jesus to tell him what happened, i.e., that John had been executed. When Jesus heard this news, he decided to withdraw with his disciples to a quiet place. Mark includes the statement by the apostles concerning the activities and results of the first mission efforts. In response, Jesus invites them to go away with him to a deserted place for rest. Luke, who does not include the story of John's death, clearly places the miracle after the first mission of the disciples. He places Jesus and the site of the miracle at or near the city of Bethsaida, which is located on the eastern side of the Sea of Galilee, so the withdrawal of Jesus appears for Luke to be an effort to provide some time for rest and reflection. The gospel of John states that Jesus went to "the other side of the Sea of Galilee" (i.e., the eastern side) and adds that the event took place near Passover time. Thus, at least some of the crowds that had been following Jesus were traveling to Jerusalem. Matthew and Mark record that when Jesus saw the crowds his response was one of compassion. According to Mark, Jesus saw the people were like sheep without a shepherd. As their spiritual shepherd, Jesus began to teach them. Luke mentions that he spoke to them about the kingdom of God and healed some. Matthew only mentions Jesus' healing ministry.

The miracle of the loaves and fishes

As it was getting late, the disciples suggested to Jesus that he send the crowd away so that they could purchase food. In response, Jesus exhorted the apostles to feed the crowd. The disciples indicated to Jesus that they only had five barley loaves and two fish. This amount of food would probably constitute someone's lunch. John adds that the food came from a boy that Andrew brought to Jesus (John 6:8-9). Jesus took that small amount of food and fed the multitude. The gospels record that after he had given thanks Jesus broke the loaves (Luke says he also broke the fish). Then he instructed that the food be distributed among the crowd, making sure everyone had enough to eat. After everyone ate, the disciples filled up twelve baskets full, probably consisting of each disciple's meal.

In a part of the world where hunger and even starvation was a daily threat to most people, a miracle of food would have been especially significant. More than that, many Jews believed that when the kingdom of God came hunger would be abolished. Some even believed that the messiah would repeat the miracle of the manna as Moses did for Israel in the wilderness. But is this why Jesus performed this miracle? The gospels are curiously silent concerning Jesus' motivation. Since Jesus performed the miracle partly in response to the disciples' concern for the people's physical welfare, one might conclude that Jesus did it to satisfy the people's hunger. However, since Jesus first challenged the disciples to feed the people and the disciples responded that such a task was impossible, it is possible that Jesus did this in part to show his disciples what was possible when a person has faith in the power of God. Mark may have suggested this interpretation when he stated that the disciples did not understand the meaning of the miracle of the loaves as an explanation for their surprise reaction to Jesus' walking on the water. Furthermore, Jesus possibly performed this miracle as a sign of the kingdom of God and he as the promised messiah.

The walking on the water (Matthew 14:22-33, Mark 6:45-52)

Introduction

Matthew and Mark record that soon after the feeding of the multitude, Jesus had made his disciples get into a boat and sail to the other side, to Capernaum. After he dismissed the crowds, Jesus went up into a mountain to pray. Matthew and Mark do not explain why Jesus did this. Matthew and Mark suggest that Jesus had concerns about his disciples. The gospel of John indicates that the people wanted to make Jesus king in Jerusalem by force (i.e., drive the Romans out and place Jesus on the throne (John 6:14-15). Based on this theory, Jesus may have withdrawn quickly to put a stop to the riot, thereby saving his ministry, his disciples' understanding, and the safety of the crowd.

Jesus on the lake

The disciples were in the middle of the lake when the winds picked up, creating a difficult and dangerous situation. Mark indicates that Jesus' coming was a result of his noticing the disciples' plight. As Jesus came toward the disciples while walking on the water, Mark states that he originally intended to pass the disciples and not get directly into the boat. Apparently, he intended to lead the disciples to safety, but the disciples were terrified, thinking he was a ghost. Jesus reassured the disciples that it was he and that they had nothing to fear.

Matthew adds that Peter asked the Lord to invite him to come to him by also walking on the water. Matthew does not explain why Peter asked Jesus to do this, except that Peter wanted to be sure this ghostly figure was really Jesus. It may also be that Peter was so impressed with Jesus' miracle that he also wanted to walk on water. By doing so, Peter would have distinguished himself among his fellow disciples. Jesus accepted Peter's challenge and invited him to walk on the water toward him. Peter then stepped out of the boat and began to walk on the water. However, Peter began to sink when he became afraid of the large waves and had to be rescued by Jesus. Only the gospel of Matthew includes this experience of Peter. This part of the story serves to demonstrate both the courageous faith and fearful doubt of Peter, which is characteristic of the spiritual life of all disciples. After Jesus entered the boat, the winds ceased blowing. Matthew notes that the disciples were astounded by what had happened and worshiped Jesus as the Son of God. In a more restrained manner, Mark simply states that the disciples were astounded because they did not perceive Jesus' supernatural power in the miracle of the loaves.

What defiles a person (Matthew 15:1-20, Mark 7:1-23)

Introduction

John notes that after the feeding of the multitude Jesus and the disciples crossed the sea to Capernaum (John 6:16-17,24,59). Matthew and Mark record that they crossed over to Gennesaret, where Jesus healed many people. Gennesaret was about 5 miles southwest of Capernaum. Since Capernaum was the more prominent town, it is likely that Jesus' discourse concerning spiritual defilement took place in Capernaum. The sayings of Jesus arose in response to questions from the scribes and Pharisees concerning Jewish purity codes. They had noticed that some of his disciples did not wash their hands before they ate. The issue was not sanitation but a religious ritual. Washing hands is not required by the Old Testament but by tradition. According to Jewish law, to be ritually clean meant that one was in a state where he or she would be permitted to worship. Uncleanness was contracted by touching certain persons, things, or by eating certain foods. Ritual impurity was contagious and transferable. Ritual washing was one way a person could be ritually purified.

Jesus' teaching of purification

In response to the Pharisees' questions, Jesus quoted a passage from Isaiah in which the prophet condemns the people for honoring human tradition over divine will. Outwardly, these people appear pious. Inwardly they are sinful, for their hearts are devoted to the legalistic traditions as much as, if not more than, the word of God itself. Jesus also pointed out how tradition can destroy the purpose of religion and divine law. As an example, Jesus cited the commandment "Honor your father and mother," as one such divine law. This law meant more than simply giving honor and respect for one's parents, but caring for them in their old age. However, sometimes people allow traditions to take on more importance than the law itself. One popular tradition was called "corban." Corban was a vow or curse, which legally meant that a person's property (i.e., money) was prohibited from benefiting the one against whom he uttered it. The purpose of corban was to encourage people to financially support the temple cult. If a person said, "My property is corban;" then he was legally prohibited from giving or using his property for any other purpose. Once a person committed his property to the temple by means of corban, then he may not use his goods for anything else, no matter how worthy. Apparently, some people had used this law in order to protect their property from family members. Under corban law, one is technically not obligated to care for one's aging parents or help the poor, so the possibility existed that one's obligation to a tradition law might prevent a person from obeying a divine law. If a tradition is allowed to have more authority than divine law, then something is very wrong. Jesus, therefore, condemned the Pharisees' tendency to elevate tradition to the same level as God's word.

What does it mean to defile a person? Jesus' answer is that defilement is not merely something outside of a person, but what is inside. External things such as food, objects, and people are not the real source of defilement, but the evil thoughts and desires that are in one's heart. In fact, sinful behavior is the result of the defilements which are within the heart. Mark notes that the practical implications of Jesus' words are that all foods are clean, meaning that the Jewish purity codes are no longer valid.

Chapter 13

Jesus the Messiah and Lord of the Church

Special Topic: The concept of messiah

In preparation for studying the account of Peter's confession at Caesarea Philippi, a brief of review some of the major ideas and terms which refer to the Jewish Messiah will be helpful. In first century Judaism, no one concept or term was universally accepted to refer to the Messiah. Instead, there were at least four terms that were commonly used: (1) The Prophet; (2) The Son of Man; (3) Messiah; (4) The Son of God.

The prophet

This term was taken from the prophecy concerning the prophet, in Deuteronomy 18, who would be like Moses. The emphasis here was more of a teaching messiah. In John 6:14, some of the people called Jesus the prophet who is to come. In Acts 3:22-26, Peter proclaimed that Jesus was the fulfillment of Deuteronomy 18:15-19:

Moses said, "The Lord your God will raise up for you from your own people a prophet like me. You must listen to whatever he tells you. And it will be that everybody who does not listen to that prophet will be utterly rooted out of the people." All the prophets, as many as have spoken, from Samuel and those after him also predicted these days.

Several texts in the Old Testament stress that Moses was unique as a prophet, for God spoke to him in a more direct way than with others (Numbers 12:5-8). Thus, a new prophet who would be like Moses would have to be similar in at least this respect. Jesus often claimed that he had an intimate relationship with God, from whom he received his teachings.

Son of man

This title primarily has its roots in Daniel 7:13, in which a person is mentioned who is described as one like a son of man. This person approaches the Ancient One who gives to him the eternal kingdom.

> "As I watched in the night visions, I saw one like a son of man [The NRSV reads "a human being"] coming with the clouds of heaven. And he came to the Ancient One and was presented before him. To him was given dominion and glory and kingship, that all peoples, nations, and languages should serve him. His dominion is an everlasting dominion that shall not pass away and his kingship in one that shall never be destroyed." (Daniel 7:13-14)

In later Jewish literature, the Son of Man was an otherworldly universal, preexistent, heavenly being. Usually he is described as the one who will appear at the end of time to execute the judgment of God and rid the world of the ungodly. This title is found on the lips of Jesus more than any other. In the gospels, only Jesus uses this title. Strangely, Jesus never explicitly calls himself "the son of man," but it is clearly implied. A study of the gospels shows that the term was used in at least three ways.

1. As a term to refer to the earthly authoritative ministry of Jesus
   ". . . the Son of Man has authority on earth to forgive sins . . . ." (Mark 2:10)
   ". . .the Son of Man is lord even of the Sabbath." (Mark 2:28)
2. As a term for the one who would suffer, die, and be raised according to God's will

"The Son of Man is going to be betrayed into human hands, and they will kill him, and on the third day he will be raised." (Matthew 17:22-23)

3. As a term for the one who will return in triumphant glory at the close of the age to judge and redeem

". . .you will see the Son of Man seated at the right hand of the Power, and coming with the clouds of heaven." (Mark 14:62)

Messiah

The word "Messiah" is a Hebrew word which means "the anointed one." The Greek word for Messiah is Christ. The term was commonly used to refer to the Messiah of nationalistic expectation. Common belief was that the Messiah would be born on earth from the line of David. He would purge Jerusalem of the heathens and destroy the godless. Additionally, the Messiah would establish the realm of the holy, where the stranger would not be admitted. Under his rule, Jerusalem would be elevated to the highest position among all the cities of the world, Israel would be restored to her former glory, and all the nations of the world would come to see her glory.

The Messiah would be a just, wise, godly, and sinless king. He would usher in an era of blessedness, prosperity, and peace. Hunger, poverty, and disease would be wiped out and prosperity and justice would reign as never before.

Son of God

Strictly speaking this is not a messianic title. Since, however, Matthew records this as part of the confession of Peter, an examination of this title is also appropriate. In the Old Testament, the expression "son of God" or something similar was used in four different ways:

1. Angels are sometimes referred to as sons of the gods (Job 1-2)
2. Quite often the king of Israel is called God's son by adoption (II Samuel 7:12-14, Psalm 89:24-29)

3. In a few places, the nation is personified as the child or first born son of God (Exodus 4:22-23, Hosea 11:1-7)
4. Israel's status as God's son was, in part, dependent on obedience, so by implication, the obedient one is God's child or son.

In Greek culture, one might use "son of God" to refer to a divine man or a god/man--a man who possesses, in a remarkable degree, genuine divine characteristics. These characteristics could be profound wisdom or supernatural power. The gospels' use of this expression is primarily dependent on the Old Testament for much of its meaning. Clearly Jesus is viewed as the Son of David, the true heir to the throne of David to establish the Kingdom. Moreover, also in several places Jesus' life seems to be compared to the nation of Israel--that he was the faithful son while Israel was unfaithful. However, in some places this title is an affirmation of his divinity as the Son of God. For example, Matthew and Luke claim that Jesus was born of a virgin, which to some extent established Jesus as God's son. Secondly, Jesus claimed that as the son he was in the closest relationship with God. This made it possible for him to reveal to humanity with authority and credibility the nature, character, and will of God.

Peter's confession (Matthew 16:13-23, Mark 8:27-33, Luke 9:16-22)

Introduction

Peter's confession of Jesus as the Messiah along with the subsequent material is a pivotal story in each of the gospels' narratives. For Matthew and Mark this event occurs halfway into the story. Before Peter's confession, the gospels narrate the story of the ministry of Jesus, the new prophet of the imminent kingdom of God. Afterwards, the focus is on Jesus' inevitable suffering and death in Jerusalem. Even Luke, who places this event earlier in his narrative, clearly interprets this event as the turning point for Jesus. From then on, his face was set toward Jerusalem.

Matthew and Mark place the story of Peter's confession after a string of brief episodes in which Jesus traveled and ministered in territory outside of Galilee, of which some were predominately Gentile territories. First, they record that Jesus and his disciples left for the region of **Tyre and Sidon**, which is in the province of Syria, and, while there, he cast out an evil spirit from the daughter of a Syrophoenician woman (Matthew 15:21-28; Mark 7:24-30). Sometime later, Jesus left there and traveled to the **Decapolis**--a region located southeast of the Sea of Galilee. His ministry there included a healing ministry (Matthew 15:29-31; Mark 7:31-37) and possibly a second feeding miracle, commonly known as the feeding of the 4000 (Matthew 15:32-39; Mark 8:1-10). After that, Jesus and the disciples sailed westward across the Sea of Galilee to **Dalmanutha**, about 10 to 15 miles south of Capernaum (Matthew 16:1-4; Mark 8:11-13). Following a brief hostile encounter with the Pharisees and Sadducees, this wandering band sailed back eastward across the sea. There Jesus instructed his disciples concerning faith, healed a blind man in **Bethsaida**, and traveled northward to the district of **Caesarea Philippi** (Matthew 16:5-13; Mark 8:14-27). Caesarea Philippi was where Jesus asked his disciples who they thought he was.

Jesus' question and the disciples' answer

Jesus raised the issue concerning the popular views concerning him. According to Mark, Jesus asked these popular views as he and the twelve disciples were "on the way," (i.e., on their journey). However, Luke points out that Jesus' question came after he had spent time in prayer. His disciples answered that most of the people considered him to be a prophet with unusual powers. Then Jesus asked the disciples a second question, and this time he wanted to know what they thought. What did his disciples believe about him? Matthew, Mark and Luke all agree that Peter answered with a confession of faith in Jesus. However, each gospel recorded a slightly different confession. Mark records, "You are the Messiah" (Christ) Luke: "The Messiah of God" Matthew: "You are the Messiah, the Son of the living God." Most likely Mark records the original confession, while Luke and Matthew add material in order to explain something of the meaning of that confession.

Following Peter's confession, Mark and Luke record that Jesus then "sternly ordered them not to tell anyone" for the Son of Man (Jesus) "must undergo great suffering, and be rejected by the elders, chief priests, and the scribes, and be killed and after three days rise again." Matthew also contains this material, but not immediately following Peter's confession. In between Peter's confession and Jesus' prediction of his future suffering, death and resurrection, Matthew has included or inserted Jesus' words concerning Peter, the rock, the building of his church, and the keys of the kingdom. Matthew is the only gospel where the word "church" appears. It appears in 16:18 and 18:17, which suggests a particular interest in the Church as a distinct religious community. The presence of this material significantly changes the tone of this narrative. In Mark and Luke, Jesus asked the disciples a question concerning himself. Peter answered Jesus with a confession of faith, and then Jesus told them not to tell anybody. However, in Matthew, when Peter answered Jesus with the confession of faith, Jesus blessed Peter for that confession, and announced that he was going to build his church over which Peter and the rest of the apostles will have some kind of authority.

The blessing of Peter, and the building of the church

Due to the importance the additional material in Matthew had in the history of Christianity, a discussion of Matthew 16:17-19 will follow. As stated above, Jesus blessed Peter because his confession was not the result of being taught by men but by his openness to God who led him to this new understanding. As part of that blessing, Jesus gave Simon the new name, Peter. When Jesus said, "You are Peter, and on this rock I will build my church;" what did he mean? What was the rock upon which the church was built? There are essentially four interpretations of the foundation rock on which Jesus would build the Church.

The rock is Peter

Simon's new name, "Peter," in Greek is actually *petros*, which usually refers to a stone, or movable rock. However, when Jesus said "and on this rock I will build my church," the word for "rock" in Greek is *petra*, and usually refers to a large ledge or immovable rock. Matthew's use of two words for "rock" would seem to argue against the belief that Jesus built the church upon Peter. Yet, it should be pointed out that when Jesus spoke these words, he probably spoke in Aramaic, a sister language to Hebrew. In Aramaic there is only one word for "rock", *kepha*, from which the name "Cephas" is derived. This name appears four times in the New Testament, each referring to the apostle Peter (John 1:42, I Corinthians 1:12; 3:22; 9:5). John 1:42 is a parallel to Matthew 16:18. It reads: "He brought Simon to Jesus, who looked at him and said, 'You are Simon son of John. You are to be called Cephas (which is translated Peter).'" When Jesus gave Simon his new name and spoke of the rock upon which the church would be built, he used the same Aramaic word for rock both times. Does that mean that Peter was the rock on which Jesus founded the Church? Not necessarily. We must remember that when Matthew translated Jesus' words from Aramaic into Greek he used two closely related words, each with a distinct meaning.

Nevertheless, Peter clearly was the leading apostle during the early days of the church. In fact, Jesus' own words in other places seem to invest some kind of leadership role for Peter (Luke 22:32 and John 21:15-19). Peter preached the first gospel sermon on the day the church was born. Most likely, Jesus was engaging in a play on words. In contemporary English, Jesus may have said, "Simon, from now on I am going to call you Rocky, but on this foundation of rock, I will build my Church." No where else in the New Testament is Peter singled out as the foundation rock for the church. Sometimes the apostles as a whole are described as a foundation, but not Peter (Ephesians 2:19-20).

The Rock is Peter's faith (i.e., faith in Jesus as the Messiah)

This interpretation emphasizes that the Church is a spiritual community which exists by the will of God and on the basis of a common faith in Jesus by all fellow members.

The Rock is the truth about Jesus

The truth about Jesus has to do with the gospel message concerning Jesus and what he did for the salvation of the world. Advocates of this view argue that the Church originally came into being and continues wherever the gospel is preached and people respond in faith.

The Rock is Jesus himself

This interpretation seems to have the most scriptural support. Jesus often spoke of himself as the chief cornerstone (Matthew 21:42, Mark 12:10, Luke 20:7). Moreover, he quoted from Psalm 118:22 (the "chief cornerstone" text) and applied the text to himself. The New Testament writers emphasized Jesus as the foundation stone of the Church (Acts 4:11,1 Corinthians 3:10-11, Ephesians 2:20, 1 Peter 2:6-7).

Jesus' Teaching Concerning the Church

In this brief passage, the reader can glean three basic concepts concerning the nature of the Church. First, Jesus and no one else is the builder of the church. Thus, the church is totally dependent on Christ for life and sustenance. Second, the Church belongs to Jesus ("my church"). He is the Church's lord and authority. Third, nothing can destroy the church. The term "Hades" means the place of the dead or death itself. However, not even death itself can destroy the Church.

Furthermore, one of the mistakes readers of this text often make is that they read into the word "church" the modern 21st century Western view of "church" as a particular religious institution with a building, organized leadership, rules for membership and faith. The English word "church" actually comes from the Greek word *kuriakon,* which original meant "the Lord's house" and often referred to a building or institution. However, the Greek word in Matthew is *ecclesia,* which means "assembly." More importantly, *ecclesia* was used to translate the Hebrew word *qahal*—a term for the congregation of Israel or the covenant people of God (Psalm 22:22). This means that Jesus' prediction of building his church was about establishing a new or renewed covenant people of God rather than a religious institution.

Binding and Loosing/the Keys of the Kingdom of Heaven

The reference to the keys suggests that Jesus was describing the apostle Peter like a gatekeeper of an ancient city. With the keys Peter can decide who will or will not enter the city. The authority to bind and loose was given to all the apostles, perhaps even the church as a whole (see Matthew 18:18), and not exclusively to Peter. To bind and loose was not a blank check to do or decide whatever one wants; those in authority have the responsibility to make decisions concerning the kingdom of God that are in keeping with the heavenly father's will.

Jesus Rebukes Peter

In Matthew, this beautiful scene of faith and blessing is followed by Jesus' troubling prediction of his suffering, death, and resurrection. In Mark and Luke, Jesus' prediction immediately follows Peter's confession of faith. This event is pivotal in the gospel story, for afterwards the story shifts to more of a focus on the prospects of Jesus' suffering in Jerusalem. In response to Jesus' words, Peter sternly rebuked Jesus for having such thoughts. He did this because his concept of messiah (a military and /or political messiah) was incompatible with the possibility of Jesus suffering disgrace and death. Without a doubt, Peter believed he was acting out of love and faith. But Peter, who was blessed for his faith, is then rebuked for his lack of faith; he has unwittingly become an instrument of Satan. Jesus' words to Satan, "Get behind me, Satan!" recall the temptation of Jesus in the wilderness. Perhaps Satan was tempting Jesus through one of his own disciples.

Implications for discipleship (Matthew 16:24-28, Mark 8:34-9:1, Luke 9:23-27)

A natural question to the serious disciple might be, "If Jesus is going to die, then what is going to happen to me? Will I have to die as well?" Most likely aware of this, Jesus discussed with his disciples what it meant to follow him. He warned them that following him meant self-denial. Losing of one's life begins with utter submission to the will of God and the needs of others. It could even mean the sacrificing of one's own life. Then Jesus asked a question: "For what will it profit them if they gain the whole world, but forfeit their life?" The word "life" is sometimes rendered "soul" in older versions. The original Greek word refers to more than simply one's physical; life, the inner and spiritual part of a person, the real self, is also included. Jesus reminded his disciples that discipleship meant being people of principle and values, people who will not compromise for short-term personal gain. Then, in order to give his disciples hope, Jesus predicted that the kingdom, in some way, would come within their lifetime. Obviously, the world is still standing. Perhaps Jesus was referring to the giving of the Holy Spirit and the establishment of the Church.

Chapter 14

From Mountain Top to Valley

The Transfiguration (Matthew 17:1-8, Mark 9:2-8, Luke 9:28-36)

About a week later, Jesus, Peter, James and John went up on a high mountain. Luke says they went up to the mountain to pray. The identity of the mountain is uncertain. Some say Mt. Nebo, and others say Mt. Hermon. Mark along with Matthew say that Jesus was transfigured there before these disciples. The Greek word translated as "transfigured" is *metamorphothei,* from which the English word "metamorphosis" comes. This word suggests that Jesus was dramatically transformed from one state of existence to another (i.e., from human to divine). In contrast, Luke simply says that "the appearance of his face changed," which can mean that Jesus' face changed in expression (e.g., from happy to sad) or that Jesus' face took on an otherworldly or divine quality. All three gospels describe changes to Jesus' clothes and face during this event. Some scholars have suggested that the bright clothes recall the appearance of an angel or some heavenly being. Matthew's description of Jesus' face may recall the portrayal of the Ancient One in Daniel 7:9-10, one like the Son of Man in Revelation 1:12-16, or may even refer to the face of Moses which glowed with God's glory after coming down from the mount (Exodus 34:29-35).

At some point, Moses and Elijah appeared with Jesus. Several explanations have been advanced for the appearance of these two Old Testament heroes. Both Moses and Elijah had important mountain top experiences with God. Both of them had strange ends to their earthly lives. Elijah was translated into heaven, and Moses died and was buried by God in a secret cave, but there was a strong tradition within Judaism that even Moses' body was translated into heaven. Most importantly, both Moses and Elijah represent key aspects of Old Testament religion, the law and the prophets. Moses was the great law giver, and Elijah was the great prophet. Moses and Elijah not only appeared with Jesus, but they were also talking with him. Luke even states that they were talking with Jesus about "his departure, which he was about to accomplish at Jerusalem." The Greek word for "departure." is *exodos*. Most likely this heavenly trio were discussing the conclusion of Jesus' work on earth; his death, resurrection, and ascension into heaven.

After a period of time had passed, Peter asked if he and the other disciples could build three booths as shelters for each of the honored guests. Luke states that Peter made this request at the time Moses and Elijah were about to leave. Peter's desire was to honor these three great leaders of God's people and preserve that moment. Mark and Luke also note that Peter was somewhat confused about what he was saying or what he should say.

After Peter finished speaking, the voice of God was heard. The gospels record that God spoke from a bright cloud which had descended and overshadowed the group. In Old Testament history, the cloud was often used by God as a symbol or vehicle of his divine and glorious presence. Probably the reason for the cloud is that it can hide or diffuse light, like the light of the sun. Thus the cloud reminds humans of the mystery that always surrounds God. Jews remembered that it was a pillar of cloud that led Israel by day. In those days, the cloud would often descend on the tabernacle and fill the most holy place. On the mount of transfiguration, the descending cloud covered the disciples, and they were afraid. The voice from the cloud reminded them that Jesus was and is more important than either Moses or Elijah. The voice, which is the voice of God, said the same words which were spoken at the baptism of Jesus when he was first declared to be the son of God. More than that, the divine voice called on all the disciples to "listen to him," (i.e., Jesus). Thus the voice of God commanded the disciples to follow Jesus and obey his words above all other human authority.

What was the purpose of the Transfiguration? Clearly, this was done at least for the spiritual benefit of the disciples. They needed a reminder concerning the unique place and authority of Jesus. However, the disciples may have also needed assurance. The gospels all note that this event took place shortly after Peter's confession and Jesus' first prediction of his death. Perhaps by getting a glimpse of the true divine glory of Jesus, God assured them that whatever suffering Jesus would have to undergo he would ultimately be victorious.

Questions concerning Elijah (Matthew 17:9-13, Mark 9:9-13)

Following the Transfiguration, the disciples began asking Jesus questions concerning Elijah. They had just seen Elijah with Moses, but they thought that Elijah was supposed to come before the coming of the kingdom of God. In part, they must have also thought that Elijah was to come before the Messiah appeared. Jesus agreed with their understanding of the prophecy, specifically Malachi 4:5-6. However, he added that Elijah had already come and that the people essentially rejected and killed him. Matthew indicates that the disciples understood that Jesus was referring to--John the Baptist. Jesus also saw a connection between how John was treated and how he, as the Son of Man, would be treated.

The healing of the boy with a spirit (Matthew 17:14-21, Mark 9:14-29, Luke 9:37-43a)

After Jesus and the disciples came down the mountain, they were greeted by a crowd and a particular man who pleaded for them to heal his son. Mark describes the boy as one who "has a spirit." Matthew used a term commonly translated as "epileptic." Literally, the Greek word translated "epileptic" means "moonstruck." The King James Version uses "lunatic," which usually suggests someone who is mentally and/or emotionally deranged. The choice of the word "epileptic" was not to suggest a clinical diagnosis but a descriptive word based on observable symptoms: sudden falling, foaming at the mouth, grinding of teeth, convulsions and/or body rigidity. Nevertheless, all the texts agree that the ultimate cause of the boy's problem was demon possession.

The father told Jesus that he had appealed to his disciples for healing, but they were unable to do it. When Jesus heard this, he was very angry at his disciples for their lack of faith which had made them unable to minister to this person. The father then appealed to Jesus and told him to do whatever he could to help his son. Jesus responded by emphasizing that all things were possible to the one who believed. The father cried out, "I believe; help my unbelief." His cry reveals the very human tendency to believe and to doubt at the same time. Then Jesus simply commanded the evil spirit to leave the boy. In response to Jesus' word, the evil spirit threw the boy into convulsions and then came out of the boy.

Amazed at what had happened, the disciples asked Jesus why they had not been able to cast out the evil spirit from the boy. Jesus explained to his disciples that prayer and faith are what make it possible to do what seem to be impossible. Jesus also reminded them that all the faith that is needed is a small amount, like size the of a mustard seed. The key is to act on the faith one has and great things can happen.

Life in the community of the kingdom of God (Matthew 18:1-35, Mark 9:33-47, Luke 9:46-50; 17:1-4; 15:3-7)

Introduction

Following the healing of the boy with a demon, the synoptics all report a second prediction by Jesus of his suffering and death, which caused great confusion and distress among the disciples (Matthew 17:22-23, Mark 9:30-32, Luke 9:43b-45). Matthew then adds a story where Jesus spoke of the temple tax. In short, Jesus told his disciples that since they were all children of the true king (God), they, like the children of earthly kings, were technically exempt from paying the tax, but that they should pay it in order not to cause offense among the Jews. The strange part of the story is that Jesus told Peter to go fishing and inside one of the fish he would find the money needed to pay the tax. However, the text never tells the reader whether Peter did this. If a miracle took place, the actual event has not been recorded. This means that the value of this story is in what Jesus said about being children of the king who are not obligated to pay taxes. Some scholars have suggested that Matthew included this story as a way of instruction to early Christians about paying taxes (Matthew 18:24-27).

The next section in Matthew is the third major discourse by Jesus, in which he addressed such topics as (1) greatness in the kingdom of heaven; (2) concern for the "little ones," the weak and struggling members on the community; (3) disciplining or rescuing the offending fellow believer; and (4) forgiving a repentant fellow believer. Mark and Luke have parallels with some of Matthew's material. Nevertheless, this study will focus primarily on Matthew 18.

Greatness in the kingdom of heaven (Matthew 18:1-5)

The discourse opens with a question from the disciples concerning greatness in the kingdom. Mark and Luke indicate that Jesus became aware of a dispute between the disciples concerning greatness. In response, Jesus placed a child in their midst and said that they must be like children in order to enter the kingdom. The particular quality of children that Jesus emphasized is humility. In Jesus' day, children were considered on the low end of the social order because they were weak, dependent, vulnerable, and without understanding; in other words, they were not self-sufficient and they knew it. To be humble is to admit that one needs God and others for life.

Concern for the little ones (Matthew 18:6-14)

There is a slight shift in the language in this section. In verses 1-5, Jesus spoke about being humble like a child as a condition for entering the kingdom. Beginning with verse 6, the word "child" is dropped for the expression "little ones." This change is more than stylistic. "Little ones" seems to refer to those in a community, such as the Church, who are spiritually and morally weak and immature. First, Jesus warned them not to do anything that could cause one of these "little ones" to stumble into sin. The metaphor of the cutting off of body parts either is a way of saying that one should do whatever it takes to avoid being such an evil influence or that people who lead others into sin should be cut off from the community of believers. Second, when one of the little ones falls into sin and wanders away, others should seek to bring him or her back. Like the shepherd who seeks the one sheep who has gone astray, so should the disciples, perhaps the entire church. In verse 10, Jesus warned the disciples not to despise any of the little ones, especially those who commit sin. They are to be like the Father in heaven who is not uncaring when one of his little ones becomes lost, but seeks them out.

Disciplining or rescuing the fellow believer (Matthew 18:15-20)

For a second time, the language shifts from "child" to "little ones" to "fellow believer" (literally "brother"). This section has traditionally been regarded as Jesus' instruction on church discipline. If discipline means the attempt to correct poor behavior, then this section is about church discipline. However, this section actually contains Jesus' instruction on how to bring back a wayward member. The oldest and best manuscripts of Matthew 18:15 do not contain the phrase "against you." When that phrase is removed from the verse, the passage changes from instruction concerning personal offenses to sins in general. Moreover, Jesus' teachings include a threefold appeal to the sinner ending with the involvement of the entire community—not likely in matters of personal offense. Therefore, this discussion will assume that Jesus' words are concerned with a member who must turn away from some particular sin.

Jesus taught that at least three appeals should be made to the sinner: a private meeting between the sinner and a concerned member; a second meeting between the sinner, the member and one or two others; and a third appeal brought to the entire church. The object of the appeals is not to condemn or punish but to persuade the person that he or she has done wrong and need to repent. If the appeal of the entire church is unsuccessful, then clearly this person no longer wants to be part of this community. In response, then, the church after much prayer, considers the person as "a Gentile and a tax collector." To say the church must consider the unrepentant in this way does not mean that the church drives him or her out of the church. Rather it means that the church acknowledges what is in fact the truth—this person has left the community of faith.

Forgiving a repentant brother or sister (Matthew 18:21-35)

While in some cases, a brother or sister will be unresponsive to every effort to bring him or her to repentance, others will admit their wrong and seek to be reconciled to God and to one's fellow disciple(s). When such a person repents and desires reconciliation, what must a disciple (or the Church) do? And if the wrong was a wrong against another fellow believer, what must that believer do? Peter's question in verse 21 addressed the second question. In a culture where personal, family, and national honor were regarded as supremely important, it would be extremely difficult for a person to continually extend forgiveness to people if they repeatedly offended him. In fact, one's honor might prevent such forgiveness. Thus, when Peter asked Jesus if he should be willing to forgive a person as much as seven times, he most likely thought he was being very generous. Rabbi Jose Ben Hanna supposedly said, "He who begs forgiveness from his neighbor must not do so more than three times." The rule of thumb of three times of forgiveness probably goes back to the repeated declaration by the Lord through Amos, "Thus says the Lord: 'For three transgressions of Damascus and even for four, I will not revoke the punishment'" (1:3,6,9,11,13; 2:1,4,6). While Peter's suggestion of seven times appeared generous, Matthew states that Jesus rejected Peter's suggestion and said, "Not seven times, but I tell you, seventy-seven times." Some translations read it as seventy times seven, but the actual number is not important. Rather, Jesus used words to convey the need for unlimited forgiveness. Jesus may have been referring to Genesis 4:24 where a certain Lamech boasted that he would take vengeance "seventy-seven fold."

In order to illustrate the need for having a forgiving heart, Jesus told a parable about a servant who owed a king a large amount of money. The ten thousand talents which this servant owed was an enormous sum, more than any one person could possibly borrow. The total tribute which the province of Galilee paid Rome for a period of 15 years might equal ten thousand talents. So the servant's request for more time in order to pay off the debt was ridiculous and unrealistic--there was no way he could pay it off. The only way he would escape the burden of the debt would be if the king simply forgave the debt, which is exactly what the king did. But when that servant met a fellow servant who owed him 100 denarii, the equivalent of about three months' wages, he neither forgave that debt nor give the man more time to pay it off. In essence, one who had received grace and mercy did not extend the same to another. The king angrily threw the first servant in prison for failing to forgive his fellow servant's debt. In somber language, the parable concludes that God will hold his people accountable for their failure to forgive one another from the heart.

This discourse opens with a call for God's people to cultivate humility in their hearts. When we practice humility, we will be concerned about others more than about ourselves. We will not despise the weak and vulnerable, but seek to rescue them from moral or spiritual danger. Moreover, we will be ready to forgive whenever a brother or sister apologizes and repents of wrongdoing. After all, God has done the same for all his people.

Chapter 15

Luke's Travel Narrative (Luke 9:51-18:14), Part 1

Introduction

Both Matthew and Mark report that following the events described above Jesus "went to the region of Judea and beyond the Jordan" (Matthew 19:1, Mark 10:1). Luke, however, states that Jesus "set his face to go to Jerusalem" (Luke 9:51). Yet Luke does not place Jesus in Jerusalem until 19:28. Between 9:51 and 19:28 is an extended narrative, which is almost completely unique to Luke. Many scholars have suggested that Luke's special material is a record of Jesus' ministry in parts of Judea and in the region beyond the Jordan known as Perea. However, Luke does not clearly inform the reader concerning the direction of Jesus' route other than that he first intended to go through Samaria. One thing seems clear. Jesus set his face to go to Jerusalem in the sense that the remainder of his ministry took on a new focus: Jesus' inevitable death and resurrection.

Jesus in Samaria (Luke 9:51-56)

Jesus apparently intended to travel to Jerusalem through Samaria. For Jews, traveling through Samaria was not common due to the long history of hostility between Jews and Samaritans. The origins of this hostility go back to the years of the exile of Israel. In 722 BC the Assyrians conquered the city of Samaria, the capital of the Northern Kingdom of Israel, and most of the conquered Jews were exiled to many places within the Assyrian empire. As a means of controlling the land, the Assyrians settled in Palestine, lived among the survivors and intermarried with the remaining Jews. The result of these marriages were the Samaritan people, a nation of mixed ancestry and religious tradition. Traditional Jews looked upon Samaritans with contempt. They were considered unclean and heretical. Thus when Jesus decided to travel through Samaria, most likely he and his disciples would be alone, since most Jews refused to travel through Samaria.

The Samaritan village to which Jesus came refused to welcome or help him. Luke records that they rejected him because his face was set toward Jerusalem. Either they resented Jesus using their land as a thoroughfare to the Jerusalem feasts, or they were upset that Jesus had not yet rejected Jerusalem and the Jews. Offended by the Samaritan reaction to Jesus, James and John requested that they send fire from heaven to destroy this village which had insulted Jesus, but Jesus refused their request and rebuked them for their vengeful attitude.

The three would-be disciples of Jesus (Luke 9:57-62)

Luke states that as Jesus and his disciples were going along the road, Jesus was approached by someone who wanted to be his disciple. Matthew, who places this event much earlier in Jesus' ministry, identifies the person as a scribe (Matthew 8:19), (probably a Jewish scribe). This first of three would-be disciples offered to follow Jesus wherever he went. Jesus responded by telling him about the hardships associated with being a disciple of Jesus. Jesus' message was that if one is to follow Jesus, he must do it on the conditions Jesus sets.

A second person also expressed a desire to follow Jesus, but only after he buried his father. Jesus' words to that person are startling: "Let the dead bury their own dead." This doesn't mean that a child should not pay final respects to his or her deceased parent. Most likely this person was saying that he wanted to follow Jesus, but first he must stay and care for his parents until they die. This means that this person might not be free to follow Jesus until it was too late. Jesus wanted this man not to make excuses but simply begin to proclaim the gospel of the kingdom.

The third person wanted to first say goodbye to his family before following Jesus. Jesus probably sensed some reluctance of the person to follow him. Therefore, Jesus insisted that one cannot be committed to one person or idea if his mind and heart are somewhere else.

The mission of the 70 disciples (Luke 10:1-24)

At the height of Jesus' popularity, Jesus must have had many followers. One indication of this is Luke's account of Jesus' commissioning of the 70 disciples. While the number twelve was a symbol of Israel, in a different way, the seventy disciples may have also been symbolic of Israel. In Exodus 24:9-11, 70 elders who assisted Moses in leading Israel are mentioned. Drawing upon that tradition, the Jewish high council, known as the Sanhedrin, consisted of about 70 men. The instructions are essentially the same as given to the 12. The results of their mission were very similar to other mission efforts by the disciples. In Luke 10:17-18, Jesus declared that the success of the disciples' mission efforts was a sign of Satan's inevitable defeat and destruction.

The parable of the good Samaritan (Luke 10:25-37)

Introduction

The parable of the good Samaritan is one of the most well-known and well-loved of all the parables of Jesus. According to Luke, the parable was given in response to a dialogue Jesus had with a lawyer. The initial question by the lawyer had to do with the requirements for eternal life. Luke said that the man was testing Jesus, so it may be that the lawyer asked this question in order to see how Jesus regarded the law of Moses. When Jesus directed the lawyer to the law of Moses, this lawyer correctly noted that the commands to love God and one's neighbor are the commands which, if followed, would lead a person to eternal life. The lawyer may have thought that Jesus' citation of the Law provided an opportunity for him to probe Jesus' thinking even more deeply by asking the follow-up question concerning the definition of the term neighbor. When the Mosaic law used the word "neighbor," it meant one's Jewish neighbor, which was the popular view at this time. Perhaps the lawyer suspected that Jesus believed that Gentiles were also one's neighbor and wanted to expose this so-called false point of view. Jesus answered him by telling this famous parable.

The Parable

The road from Jerusalem to Jericho was about 17 miles long, descending about 3000 feet. The road was narrow, rocky, and notorious for bandits. The parable states that a traveler was attacked, beaten and robbed. Representatives from the religious leadership of Israel—a Levite and a priest--saw the man but passed by on the other side. No reason is given for their actions. They may have thought that the man was already dead, and if they were to touch the corpse, they would become ceremonially unclean. Perhaps one or both of them were afraid that it was a trap set by would-be bandits, or they simply may have been unconcerned about the man's condition. At this point in the story, Jesus' audience was probably following the story very closely, anticipating the hero to be some other type of Jew. But Jesus surprised them by making the hero a Samaritan. The Samaritan traveler helped the man, and even nursed him back to heath. It was this Samaritan who showed compassion and mercy to a Jew. This fact forced the lawyer to admit that only the Samaritan had acted as a neighbor. Thus, while the lawyer had inquired as to who was his neighbor, Jesus responded by pointing out that one must consider oneself a neighbor to anyone who needs help.

Mary and Martha (Luke 10:38-42)

Luke next records that Jesus entered a certain village where Mary and Martha lived. John says that Mary and Martha lived in Bethany with their brother, Lazarus (John 11:1). Martha is described as having the dominant role since she invited Jesus to stay with her, and she proceeded to attend to his needs. Her sister, Mary, however, simply sat at Jesus' feet to listen to his words. Believing Jesus was insensitive to her feelings and needs, Martha complained to Jesus because he did not tell Mary to help Martha with the housework, but rather allowed her to simply listen to him. Jesus responded by reminding Martha that the spiritual benefits Mary was receiving were more important than the work Martha was doing because Jesus' instructions can lead Mary to great faith and knowledge of God. Jesus' lesson to Martha was about setting the right priorities. In addition to this, by his actions, Jesus broke a long-standing social custom against the teaching of women by rabbis. In fact, Jesus clearly implied that women could be his disciples as well as men.

Teaching on prayer (Luke 11:1-13)

Introduction

Prayer is a favorite topic for Luke. In this section, Luke presents a shorter version of the Lord's Prayer and a parable concerning prayer. According to Luke, Jesus gave this teaching in response to his disciples' request for him to teach them to pray. Obviously, the disciples had been praying for a long time, since prayer was a part of Jewish piety. Their request must have had something to do with having the proper attitude concerning prayer.

The Lord's Prayer

Luke's shorter version is very similar to the longer one in Matthew. However, Luke's version may give more emphasis concerning the need to trust in God to supply one's needs. This same theme is elaborated in the parable which follows.

Parable of the Friend at Midnight

This is a parable about persistence in prayer. The setting for the parable is a typical Middle Eastern home where the family are all sleeping together in the same room. When the friend came knocking on his neighbor's door requesting bread, the neighbor initially refused because doing so would probably disturb the entire household. The parable notes that the friend eventually got bread from his neighbor because he continued to knock and ask until his neighbor got up to give him some. So also, people who pray persistently about something will receive blessings from God.

The parable of the rich fool (Luke 12:13-21)

Introduction

According to Luke, Jesus warned against the hypocrisy of the Pharisees (12:1), and then called on his disciples to boldly take a stand for him in the face of opposition (12:2-12). Following this, Luke records that a man in the audience apparently interrupted Jesus to ask him to settle a dispute between this man and his brother concerning an inheritance. Jesus refused to do this and, apparently, was not pleased with the man. He said that his mission was not to settle financial disputes. He also exhorted the man and the crowd to avoid covetousness because a person's life consisted of more than material possessions.

The parable

Jesus then told a parable about a rich man. This rich man experienced a bumper crop. After he realized just how large the crop would be, he asked himself, "What shall I do?" His barns were already full. The solution to the rich man's dilemma was to build more and bigger barns in order to store all his grain for himself. He apparently gave no thought to using his wealth for others. Note the prominent use of the pronouns "I," "me," "my," "mine." His entire thinking was self-centered. The rich man apparently thought even his soul would be taken care of by these possessions. In addition, he also thought he would live a long time. Then in the midst of his success, God's judgment came to him in death. God called him "fool." He told him that life is more than food and clothes. The rich man also learned that no one had absolute control of the future. No one knows how long he or she will live, and so God told him that his life was soon to be over, and that all his riches would go to others without his consent.

The point of the story

Unlike other parables, the moral of this parable is that fools pile up earthly riches for themselves but neglect their relationship with God--their spiritual life. Thus a self-centered life is a life apart from God.

A call to repentance (Luke 13:1-9)

In Luke 12:49-59, Jesus proclaimed that his ministry would bring disturbance in people's lives. He described his mission as bringing fire on the earth and that he came to bring division, even division within households. The point of Jesus' words was not that he came to break up families and friendships, but that his ministry and preaching would be of such a nature that people would be forced to enthusiastically embrace it or oppose it. Jesus then accused the crowd of spiritual blindness to the present situation, the coming of the kingdom of God. Finally, Jesus warned them they must become right before the divine judge or else suffer punishment.

In response, some of the people told Jesus of the murder of the Galileans, assuming that his words were particularly important. The Galileans were a fierce nationalist Jewish group often associated with the Zealots. According to Josephus, a certain Judas the Galilean started the Zealots. The incident referred to by these people is unknown, but apparently some of the people believed that the Galileans had deserved to die. Their death was seen as punishment from God. However, Jesus said that these dead Galileans were no worse than the Galileans who survived. Suffering is not always the result of God's punishment. Then Jesus said that unless they repented they would also perish. He may have been thinking of the future destruction of Jerusalem.

As another illustration, Jesus added a second incident, in which the tower of Siloam fell on some Jews, killing 18 of them. The tower may have been a Roman construction project. Apparently some had concluded that the 18 Jews who died were killed by God for working for the ungodly Romans. Again Jesus refused to accept the opinion that these dead Jews were worse sinners than the survivors. Jesus stressed that unless the people repent, they would perish.

In order to further emphasize the people's need for repentance, Jesus told a parable about a fig tree. In this parable, the man who planted a fig tree is God, and the fig tree is probably Israel or Jerusalem. According to the parable, after a period of three years, the man looked for fruit on the tree, but found nothing. Three years is the normal time for a fig tree to mature and bear fruit. If it hasn't by then, it probably won't, so the owner regarded the tree as useless and thus decided that the tree should be cut down so it would not continue to use up the good soil. The vine dresser, who apparently represented Jesus, pleaded that the owner give him one additional year in which he (the vine dresser) would give very special care to this tree. He planned to dig around the tree to provide a better irrigation system for it, and to fertilize the tree, something rarely done in Palestine. If these measures worked, then the owner finally would have a fruit-bearing tree, but if the measures did not work, then the tree would be cut down and thrown away.

In this parable, Jesus taught that God had been extremely patient with his people, even giving them additional opportunities to repent and be saved. In view of God's patience, it is important that his people be a productive people, using what God has given them for good and for others. However, one should keep in mind that there is a final opportunity after which it is too late to repent.

Chapter 16

Luke's Travel Narrative, Part 2

Jesus at a banquet (Luke 14:1-24)

Introduction

The rest of Luke 13 contains a story of Jesus healing a crippled woman on the sabbath, which is loosely connected to the parables of the mustard seed and the yeast, sayings concerning divine judgment and the coming kingdom of God, Jesus' response to the threat of Herod Antipas, and his lament over Jerusalem. Chapter 14 opens on the Sabbath with Jesus at the home of a Pharisee for a meal. During the meal, a man suffering from dropsy, a swelling from an abnormal collection of fluids in the body, approached Jesus. Again Jesus was faced with the test of whether or not he should heal on the sabbath. Jesus' words to the Pharisee and his guests were almost the same as the ones said when he healed the man with the withered hand. His words and action left them speechless (14:1-6).

Jesus' Teaching on Humility (Luke 14:7-14)

At this same dinner, Jesus became aware of the dinner guests,' efforts to have the seats of honor, so Jesus told a parable concerning humility. As

Luke has preserved it, the saying is not technically a parable. Luke may have used the term "parable" to mean an illustration. However, perhaps there originally was a parable about people at a dinner party. The parable may have been something like the following.

Two men were invited to a banquet. The first man entered the banquet and immediately sought out the most prominent seat at the banquet. The second man also came to the banquet and took the lowest seat, grateful for just being invited. When the host of the banquet entered the room, the host noticed the man sitting in the seat of honor. Angered by the man's boldness to take upon himself this honor, he ordered the man to get up from that seat and to move to one of the lowest seats, but when the host saw the second man sitting in the lowliest seat, he invited the man to move up near him to a seat of honor.

Jesus' lesson was that one who tries for the honored seat at the dinner table will be embarrassed when he or she is forced to a lower seat. So in order to avoid embarrassment, one should take a lower seat, for honor may come to the one who is then asked to sit at the seat of honor. Of course, Jesus was not only commenting on table manners, nor is it the primary lesson. The point is that self-exaltation is the opposite of the requirements for the kingdom; rather, humility is part of kingdom life.

Surprisingly, Jesus then instructed his hosts concerning whom they should invite to a banquet. The issue had to do more with the people's motivations for inviting someone to a banquet. Some people do good to others hoping they will receive something similar from those they helped. When Jesus told them to invite the poor, blind and lame, he was telling them to do good to people who could not or probably would not pay them back. Thus, one does good expecting nothing in return. In addition, Jesus' words call people to show more concern for the poor.

Parable of the great dinner (Luke 14:15-24)

One of the guests commented on the future blessings of the Messianic banquet. In response to this, Jesus told a parable about invitations to a banquet. Jesus said that a man invited people to a banquet. When everything for the banquet was ready, the servants were sent to call people to come to the banquet. However, each of the guests excused him or herself for various reasons. When the host learned that his invitations had been rejected by the guests, he ordered that the invitations be extended to the common people, who readily accepted. Additionally, invitations were sent to anyone who would come.

This was a parable of warning to the Pharisees not to reject Jesus, or they might lose the kingdom. Since the kingdom was already present in the person and work of Jesus, the Jewish leaders' rejection of Jesus would actually be a rejection of the Kingdom.

The cost of discipleship (Luke 14:25-35)

The setting in Luke changed from a banquet to a great crowd who were following Jesus. Aware that many in the crowd wanted to be his disciples, Jesus told them the price they would have to pay. Jesus first addressed the implications for one's family relations. He told the people that they must hate one's family members as a condition of following him. The word "hate" does not mean negative and hostile feelings. In fact, Jesus always taught his disciples to love all people. Jesus used the word "hate" because it was an extreme word to depict the difference in the kind of relationship one should have with God in distinction from other relationships. In the Old Testament, "hate" used to refer to a radical and emotional choice of preference (Genesis 29:30-31, Malachi 1:2-3). Jesus was also not calling for self-hatred. Instead, this was another way of saying that one must renounce ownership of all that he or she has or is. Unless a person is willing to do this, Jesus says that person "cannot be my disciple" The verb "cannot" means that one is unable or not capable of being Jesus' disciple. Thus, nothing or no one must come before one's responsibilities to God.

With this in mind, Jesus exhorted the crowds to "carry the cross." A more literal translation would be "bear his own cross." The cross always meant crucifixion, a horrible form of death, a supreme experience of humiliation and forsakenness. Previously, Jesus had told the disciples that they must share in his ministry. Where he would go, they must go. If he must suffer, they must be willing to suffer as well. The cross symbolizes radical self-denial, so discipleship means forsaking all self-seeking efforts.

Jesus' teaching on the cost of discipleship presents a very serious picture concerning the implications of following Jesus. In fact, the personal price for each disciple is so high that one should not become a disciple flippantly or without thought. The following parables very aptly illustrate the need for a person to count the cost before becoming one of Jesus' disciples. The first parable is usually called The Man Building a Tower. The point of the parable is that it is foolish to begin a project if one won't be able to finish. A person needs to start a project with the assurance that he can complete it. Disciples must not be quitters. The next parable, The King Going to War, teaches a message very similar to the first one. However, there is one difference: One can choose to build a tower or not, but the king whose land has been invaded must do something. He must calculate which course of action would be best--war or terms of peace. The exhortation of the parable of the tower is that a person should make the effort to decide whether he can afford to follow Jesus. On the other hand, the parable about the king challenges the hearer to determine if he can really afford not to follow Jesus. In both parables, Jesus instructed the crowds that becoming a disciple is serious business and should not be done unless one is truly committed to Jesus, for Jesus demands that a person renounce all.

Parables of the Lost Sheep and Lost Coin (Luke 15:1-10)

Background of the parables

In Luke 14:15-24, Jesus told a parable about a great banquet where the invited guests did not come, so people off the streets were invited. Afterwards, Jesus told the following crowds that he demands true and full commitment as a condition of discipleship (Luke 14:25-35). Despite Jesus' hard call for discipleship, Luke reports that the tax collectors and sinners apparently had responded to Jesus' message and were coming to him (15:1-2). When they saw this taking place, the Pharisees and scribes were horrified and criticized Jesus for accepting these people. In response to these criticisms, Luke records that Jesus told the following parables. These stories were designed to explain that Jesus' association with tax collectors and sinners was really an expression of God's love. Some scholars have suggested that Jesus may not have spoken all of these parables one at a time in this setting, but that Luke brought together three parables which communicated a similar message. These three parables will be examined in this section.

Parable of the lost sheep

According to the parable, a man who had 100 sheep lost one sheep. Because that one sheep was important to the shepherd, he left the flock to find the lost one. Not only did the shepherd search for the one sheep, he would not stop looking until he found the sheep. Eventually, the shepherd found the sheep and rescued it. Instead of punishing the sheep for wandering astray, the shepherd placed the sheep on his shoulders and rejoiced with his neighbors for the safe recovery of the sheep. The point of the story is this: The return of one sinner to God is more cause for rejoicing in heaven than for all the faithful. It is only because of the initiative of the seeking God that any person has hope of salvation. Thus Jesus was doing the work of God.

Parable of the lost coin

Here Jesus switched from the field to a domestic setting. Jesus said that a woman lost a silver coin. This coin may have been part of a headdress of ten silver coins that a woman would wear on special occasions as a sign of her married state. The woman searched the house thoroughly until she found the coin. When she found the coin, there was great rejoicing. In a similar way, the angels in heaven rejoice when one sinner repents.

Like the examples of the shepherd and the woman, Jesus viewed his ministry to include seeking out the lost and bringing them back. God is, therefore, a seeking God, one who takes the initiative. The rescue of the sheep and the coin was due to the work of the shepherd and the woman. Similarly, Jesus was willing to associate with the sinners because they were the lost sheep. Thus Jesus' ministry was an indictment of the ministry of many Pharisees who refused to associate with such people until they repented.

Parable of the lost son (Luke 15:11-32)

Introduction

This is the third and final parable in Jesus' defense of his ministry. This parable is probably the most well-known and loved of all the parables of Jesus. It is also the longest and most complex. There are three theological themes in the parable: (1) the sin and repentance of the son; (2) the overwhelming love of the father; (3) the self-righteous attitude of the elder son. The narrative was probably a very familiar one; a loving father, a rebellious younger brother and a faithful older son. One interesting parallel with this parable is the story of Jacob and Esau, twin brothers, who contested over the inheritance from their father, Isaac(Genesis 27-33). In the biblical account, the younger Jacob tricks his aging father into giving him the first born's blessing and the inheritance. Consequently, he is forced into exile for over 20 years, after which he returns and is reconciled with his older brother, Esau. Whether the younger brother is ever reconciled with his elder brother in the parable is left unresolved.

The parable

In this parable, the younger of two sons demanded from their father his share of the inheritance. While not legally obligated to grant such a request, the father granted his son's demand. The son then left for a far country where he wasted his entire fortune on loose living. When a famine hit, the younger son had nothing and no one. In desperation, he hired himself out to feed swine, which would have been distasteful and humiliating for a Jew. This son must have felt that he had sunk to the lowest possible place in life.

In the midst of his trouble, the younger man came to grips with his actions. When he came to his senses, he realized the extent of his sin, the greatness of his need, and the source of his strength. He decided to go back home and ask his father only for a position as one of his servants, since he felt unworthy to be reinstated as a son.

The story implies that the father was continually looking for his son to return. When he finally saw him, he did not wait until his son actually reached the hourse. He saw him at a distance and ran out to meet him. In humility, the son humbly confessed his guilt and unworthiness. But the father, out of love, would not let his son finish. Instead of reproaching or punishing his son, the father ordered his servants to place a robe, a ring, and sandals on his son. Then the father announced a feast to celebrate the son's return.

However, when the elder brother heard the music, he drew near the house, perhaps suspecting what it meant. He learned his brother had returned and the father was honoring him, but he refused to join in the celebration. The father sought to persuade him to come in. This indicates that the father loved both sons, but the elder brother refused, and said the following:

1. "I have been working like a slave for you." He saw his relationship with his father more like that of a slave with a master than a son with a father.
2. "I have never disobeyed your command." The elder son claimed that he was the model son, the one who never crossed the line into rebellion.
3. "You have never given me even a young goat so that I might celebrate with my friends." The son stated that he had done so much for his father but had never been appreciated for all his work. He felt that it was an injustice for his younger brother, whom he accused of sin, to be honored when he had never been honored by the father.

The father responds:

1. He acknowledges and possibly expresses appreciation for the elder son's faithfulness. "You are always with me"
2. "All that is mine is yours." All the father's possessions were at his disposal to be used at his discretion. In essence, he says that his elder son could have had a party and can still enjoy the blessings from the storehouse of the father's wealth.
3. The father insists that it is also right to honor and encourage the younger son because he is home safe and sound.

The message of the parable can be gleaned at several levels, originally to the Pharisees, and then to all. First, Jesus taught that God loves the sinner and wants him or her back. Second, when a sinner repents and comes back to the fold, the faithful are to be thankful that someone was able to bring them back. Thirdly, every believer is invited to share in the joy of God by going out to search for the lost, and then leading them back home.

Chapter 17

Luke's Travel Narrative, Part 3

The parable of the dishonest steward (Luke 16:1-13)

A fourth consecutive parable is found in Luke 16 concerning a dishonest steward. While the setting and theme of this fourth parable is quite different from the previous three, there may be a connection between the parable of the lost son and the one about the dishonest steward. Both of them refer to the wasting of goods.

The parable opens with an absentee lord who had set a steward in charge of his estate. Unfortunately, the steward was irresponsible in his use of the lord's property. As a result, the owner dismissed him for his mismanagement. Having become unemployed, the former steward faced a predicament. He was essentially too weak and lazy to do manual labor and was too proud to beg, so he was forced to take action in order to survive. He decided to go to individuals who borrowed money or goods on credit from his former master. Then he allowed them to destroy their old contracts and sign new ones in which they could pay off their debts at a discount price. Most likely the former steward intended to keep the money. He thus robbed his master and gained favor from the debtors. The former master suspected what had happened, but could not prove it. However, the owner grudgingly admired and praised the former steward for his cleverness.

This is probably the strangest of all Jesus' parables since the so-called hero of the story is a dishonest steward, who used deception and dishonesty to accomplish his goal. The steward is not to be honored for his dishonesty but for his cleverness or cunning. The lesson of the parable is that followers of Jesus should be just as wise and cunning as are worldly people. Jesus' disciples must use their money for spiritual purposes just as wisely as the world uses its wealth for their selfish aims. Faithfulness in little things will determine one's fitness to handle larger and more important things.

The rich man and Lazarus (Luke 16:19-31)

Introduction

This story is about greed, insensitivity, and judgment. Though most of the story takes place in the other world, the lesson is concerned about life in this world. There is the implied exhortation to be compassionate and giving in response to the needs of others. In chapters 14 and 15, Jesus spoke about the need to reach out to the poor and lost for God's kingdom. The subject in chapter 16 is money. The parable of the unrighteous servant depicts a person's astuteness with money. Following that, Luke referred to the Pharisees as lovers of money. The story of the rich man and Lazarus combines the subject of wealth with the need for compassion.

The two as they appeared in this world

The rich man is described as one who wore purple and fine linen, which may imply either royalty or the priesthood. In addition to his dress, Luke states that the rich man sumptuously dined every day to an extent that approached gluttony. In stark contrast, Lazarus is portrayed as a poor beggar, covered with sores. He was so weak and helpless that he could not drive away the street dogs who bothered, if not threatened, him. He was so hungry that he desired the crumbs off the master's table. These crumbs may have been a thin flat type bread, which was also used as a type of napkin.

The two in the other world

After his death, Lazarus was carried by angels to be with Abraham. In other words, Lazarus was honored by God in death and taken to a place of glory and peace--a place where he could recline next to Abraham at a heavenly feast. Again, in complete contrast, the rich man also died but was buried and then taken to a place of torment. In the after world, there was a complete reversal of roles between Lazarus and the rich man. The one who had everything good now had nothing good, and the one who had nothing good now had everything good. Yet, even in this new situation, the rich man still acted as if he were superior to Lazarus. He requested that Lazarus be sent down to cool his tongue. Later, he asked if Lazarus could be sent back to earth to warn his brothers. Nevertheless, his situation was completely hopeless, for he was separated from God, by a deep fixed chasm. His judgment was final.

Aware of the hopelessness of his state, he pleaded that someone warn his brothers. Abraham argued there had been sufficient warning in Scripture, and his brothers had repeatedly ignored the warnings. The rich man then felt his brothers needed a miracle, such as a resurrection, to persuade them, but Abraham replied that since they had rejected the Scriptures, not even a resurrection would convince them to have faith and repent.

The lessons of the parable

The primary lesson of this parable is that **riches do not guarantee acceptance with God nor are they necessarily a blessing for righteousness.** In this story, the poor man was saved while the rich man was condemned. While not explicitly stated, most likely the rich man was condemned for maintaining a self-indulgent lifestyle with no care for the poor. There also may be some secondary lessons or information concerning the typical Jewish belief in the afterlife. First, this parable assumes that at death the soul of an individual will go to a place of the dead. Normally, the Jews referred to this place as Sheol. The Greek word Hades, which appears in this story, was adopted by Greek-speaking Jews as the Greek equivalent to Sheol. Second, this parable also assumes that this place of the dead had a place of blessing and reward for the righteousness, and a place of torment and punishment for the unrighteousness. Lazarus' reward is to be with Abraham. Literally, this reward is called "Abraham's Bosom." The place of torment is either unnamed or is called Hades. Third, Jews believed that the dead would remain in these places until the Last Day, the day of resurrection. In other words, it was an interim place. Fourth, the great chasm between the good and bad places signified that at death a person's eternal destiny was fixed. No second chance was available. This was also a part of Jewish belief. Fifth, some are items in this story are simply included for dramatic effect and do not represent reality as the Jews understood, such as the references to water, fire, fingers, and tongue.

Jesus' comments concerning the coming of the Kingdom (Luke 17:20-37)

The message of John the Baptist and Jesus had been that the kingdom of God was at hand. Such a message would naturally cause curiosity about the actual timing of its coming, so the Pharisees raised a question concerning the coming of the kingdom. Jesus' answer was not what they expected. He said that the kingdom would not come with signs to be observed. Neither would the kingdom be located at any particular place. Instead, he said, "The kingdom of God is among you," The future becomes the present. It is already here! The Greek phrase translated "among you" may also be rendered "in the midst of you" or simply "in you." Each translation suggests a different meaning of Jesus' words. If Jesus said "among you," then he probably meant that the kingdom was present in the faithful believing community. If Jesus meant "in the midst of you," he most likely was claiming that the kingdom of God could be seen in his life and ministry. Finally, the phrase "in you" suggests that the kingdom is a spiritual reality. While the New Testament seems to support all three interpretations, most likely Jesus had in mind his own life and ministry as evidence for the kingdom.

Luke then connects these words of Jesus to the Pharisees with instruction to his disciples concerning the days of the Son of Man, the time of divine judgment on the earth. Much of this material is also found in Matthew's account of Jesus' Olivet Discourse (Matthew 24), which will be discussed at length later in this study. In this discourse, Jesus said that there will come a time when the faithful will long for the coming of the Son of Man (Messiah), but they will need patience. The coming of Christ is certain but unknown as to when he will appear. Prior to the Son's glorious return, he must endure rejection and great suffering, an allusion to Jesus' crucifixion. After the suffering is over, the Son of Man, having been raised from the dead and exalted to the right hand of God, will return at a time when people are carrying on their normal routines of life. In preparation for this day, each person should seek to free him or herself from the selfish attachments of earthly possessions and give his or her heart and life first to God and his kingdom. On that day, a separation of people will occur, an indication of divine judgment. Jesus concluded this saying with a proverb about vultures. Many of the older English translations read "eagles" instead of "vultures." However, the mention of a corpse makes it more probable that "vultures" is the correct reading. The point of the proverb is that judgment cannot be averted any more than vultures can be kept away from a corpse. It may also mean that the day will happen when the conditions are right.

The parable of the widow and judge (Luke 18:1-8)

Introduction

Luke seems to connect the following parable with Jesus' teachings concerning the second coming of the Son of Man and divine judgment. The parable is about someone who sought justice and vindication and persisted in that quest until justice was given. The people of God sometimes must live with suffering and injustice. When that happens, they must choose whether they will simply give up hope or continue to believe that God will one day deliver them. This parable is about persistence in prayer to a responsive God.

The parable

There are two main characters in this parable, a judge and a widow. The judge is described as one who cared neither for God nor people. The parable was probably not referring to a Jewish judge. Ordinarily, Jewish disputes were taken to the elders and not to court. This judge probably was a paid magistrate who had been appointed by the Romans or a local ruler. These judges were well known for their willingness to make quick decisions if the bribe was right. The official name for the position was *Dayyaneh Gezeroth*, which means "judges of prohibitions and punishments." However, the local people often called them *Dayyaneh Gezeloth*, which means "robber judges." The other main character was the widow. In the first century, the widow was the symbol for the poor and defenseless. This widow is described as one who sought out justice for herself. Jesus states that she kept coming back to court to plead her case before the judge, and would not let the matter rest until action was taken.

Eventually, the judge had to give her justice. The parable makes it clear that the judge's motives for helping her had nothing to do with his desire for justice. Instead, Luke states that he vindicated her to get rid of her because she had become a real pest. In fact, the judge had said to himself: "I will grant her justice, so that she may not wear me out by continually coming." When the judge spoke of her wearing him out, the original Greek could mean that the widow might actually give him a black eye. Because she was so persistent in her pursuit, the widow eventually received justice.

Jesus' lesson is that if an unjust judge will eventually respond favorably to one's request, will not the loving God respond to his people in an even greater way? This is an exhortation for godly people never to give up believing and praying. One should not despair because an answer to prayer hasn't come immediately. Persistence shows true desire and faith. However long it takes, persistent prayer will be answered. The promise that God will vindicate the people of God quickly probably refers more to the certainty of the vindication rather than simply to the time. In other words, God will deliver the faithful quickly, suddenly, and surely.

The parable of the tax collector and pharisee (Luke 18:9-14)

Luke indicates that Jesus told the parable of the Pharisee and the tax collector to those who took pride in their own righteousness and despised others whom they considered less righteous. He placed this parable immediately after the parable about the widow and the judge because prayer is an important feature in both.

The parable describes two men who went up to the temple to pray. The Pharisee is said to have prayed with himself and not to God. To some extent, the Pharisee's prayer was really a celebration of his piety, even to the extent that he exceeded the legal requirements of the law concerning fasting and tithing. He even compared himself with the so-called lesser men. In particular, the Pharisee expressed gratitude that he was not a sinner like the tax collector (publican) who apparently was near him. Probably everything he said was true, but in his prayer, this man does not give thanks or glory to God for all he has and is. He also did not confess any weakness or sins nor ask for mercy and forgiveness.

On the other hand, the tax collector prayed very differently. There was no list of achievements to prove his righteousness before God and others. Instead, his humility and guilt would not even let him look up to heaven. This prayer was not full of self-congratulation. Instead, it was a simple prayer for divine mercy from one who knew too well his own sinfulness before God. This man, Jesus said, was justified or acquitted of his sins.

In this parable, Jesus taught that pride will make meaningless one's prayer and threatens one's relationship with God. Furthermore, God will have no regard for someone's worship, including prayer, if he or she persists in neglecting and/or mistreating other people. True prayer and religion must be done humbly, realizing one's constant need of God's mercy and strength.

Chapter 18

The Journey of Jesus to Jerusalem

Luke's special material ends with the conclusion of the parable of the Pharisee and the tax collector in 18:14. At this point, Luke returns to the chronological sequence of Mark. This section includes material concerning events which took place in Judea while Jesus and the disciples were traveling to Jerusalem. The first unit, however, is found only in Matthew and Mark: Jesus' teaching of marriage and divorce.

Marriage and divorce (Matthew 19:3-12)

Both Matthew and Mark state that the Pharisee asked Jesus a question in order to test or trap him. The issue had to do with the legal cause or grounds for divorce. The question was how to interpret the Mosaic Law in Deuteronomy 24:1:

> Suppose a man enters into marriage with a woman, but she does not please him because he finds something objectionable about her, and so he writes her a certificate of divorce, puts it in her hand, and sends her out of his house; she then leaves his house and goes off to become another man's wife. Then suppose the second man dislikes her, writes

> her a bill of divorce, puts it in her hand, and sends her out of his house (or the second man who married her dies); her first husband, who sent her away, is not permitted to take her again to be his wife after she has been defiled; for that would be abhorrent to the Lord, and you shall not bring guile on the land that the Lord your God is giving you as a possession.

The issue centered around the expression "something objectionable" or "uncleanness" or "unclean thing." The rabbinical school of Hillel interpreted this to be any number of things, even to such an insignificant cause as burning the bread. The rabbinical school of Shammai interpreted this same word in Deuteronomy to mean adultery. Among the Jews, only men had the right of divorce.

Jesus responded by pointing to the divine will for marriage. He went back to the creation account in Genesis 1 and 2 to show the original ideal for marriage. From these texts, Jesus emphasized three basic characteristics of marriage. First, God created marriage. It is God who joins the two together. Second, marriage was instituted to form a oneness, a relationship for equals in partnership. Third, marriage was intended to be a lifetime relationship.

In response, the Pharisees claimed that if Jesus was right, why did Moses allow for divorce? Was Jesus ignoring or violating the Law? Jesus answered that Moses allowed for divorce as a concession to human sinfulness. Before the Law, divorce was rampant, which meant that women were completely at the mercy of their husbands. Women at that time were completely dependent on a male authority (husband, father, brother) for support. They could not initiate a divorce, nor could they stop one, for they had no real legal standing. Thus the Mosaic law was given to curb a bad situation. A man could divorce his wife, but he could not take her back after she had been the wife of another. In essence, the law gave some initial protection of women from the capriciousness of some men. Nevertheless, the original intent of God for marriage was that marriage should be a lifetime relationship.

Mark's version does not include any exception clause, but adds the possibility that a woman could divorce her husband. Such a statement would have been unthinkable to Jews, but in Rome, it was a real possibility, especially for women of high standing. Many scholars have suggested that Mark was written in Rome to primarily Roman Christians, and the evangelist must have modified this saying of Jesus in such a way to be meaningful for Roman Christians. Whatever the truth of these theories, Roman Catholic authorities have used this reading in Mark to stress that there are no grounds for divorce, not even adultery. Luke also does not include the exception clause.

There are many different interpretations concerning divorce and remarriage. The primary question, however, is what were Jesus' intentions when he gave this teaching? Was he setting forth a new law? Was he simply siding with the conservative wing of the Pharisees? Was he laying down principles for the purpose of correcting and preventing serious marital problems? We should remember that the Pharisees asked Jesus about grounds for divorce, and Jesus essentially answered by telling them what was God's will for marriage.

Jesus and children (Matthew 19:13-15, Mark 10:13-16, Luke 18:15-17)

Jews considered children as special blessings from God, yet children had virtually no rights. Children were usually placed on the lowest level of the social order, since they were weak, naive, helpless, and dependent on others. Apparently, some parents were impressed with Jesus, so they brought their children to him in order that he might bless them. The disciples rebuked the parents for doing this. They may have thought that the Master was too dignified to spend time with children. They also may have thought that the children were or might become an interruption just as Jesus was about to give some important lesson.

When he became aware of what the disciples were doing, Jesus was indignant at the them for their exclusiveness and snobbery. He wanted the children to come. He said that the Kingdom of God belongs to children. Traditionally this has meant that a childlike quality must be present in the lives of people who desire to be in the Kingdom. Perhaps this means that disciples must demonstrate a childlike trust in God. Others have suggested that it means disciples must be genuine, not hypocritical. In Matthew 18:4, Jesus said that one must have humility like a child in order to be in the kingdom. Following this, Jesus received the children, took them into his arms, and blessed them.

Jesus and the rich man (Matthew 19:16-30, Mark 10:17-31, Luke 18:18-30)

A rich man came to Jesus and asked him what he must do to have eternal life. Mark, who understands discipleship as a journey, mentions that the man came to Jesus as he was about to set out on the road. Matthew and Luke provide no clear context for this event, except that Luke adds that the man was a ruler. Mark also states that the rich man ran up and knelt before Jesus, an act of genuine humility. Then, according to Mark, the rich man addressed Jesus as "good teacher." Jesus responded by asking him, "Why do you call me good? No one is good but God alone." Jesus apparently was concerned that the young man was using the word "good" in a thoughtless or superficial manner. By saying that only God is good, Jesus was not denying his own divinity but reminding the man that to address someone as good implies that that person either comes from God, is extremely close with God, or is, in fact, divine himself. In slight contrast, Matthew records that the young man asks Jesus what good deed must he do to gain eternal life. Matthew stressed a good deed instead of a good teacher. Could the man have used the word "good" twice? Not likely. Jesus' answer in Matthew and Mark is very similar. One suggestion given by scholars is that the man probably addressed Jesus as a good teacher and that Matthew, not wanting his readers to conclude that Jesus was not good and therefore not divine, modified the question to refer to good works. Jesus stated that only by keeping the Law, especially the Ten Commandments, could the man gain eternal life.

The man answered that he had faithfully kept the Law since his youth, yet he still lacked something. While Mark and Luke record that Jesus informed the man of his lack, Matthew wrote that the man was acutely aware of his moral and spiritual deficiencies. In reply, Jesus said that the man would find what he was looking for if he were to sell all his possessions, give them away to the poor, and then follow him. This is the only time where Jesus made such a requirement for someone. Perhaps money and possessions were a problem for this man. Riches in the ancient world were often a symbol of one's dignity, righteousness, and power in the community. Therefore, if one were to take away those riches, that person would be reduced to being a simple human being. Unfortunately, the man walked away sorrowfully because he couldn't give up that which had been part of him since birth.

When Jesus saw the rich man leave, he reflected on the power material wealth can have on a person. He used the exaggerated illustration of a camel going through the eye of a needle to say that it would be very difficult for a rich man to be saved--to give up that which defined him and gave him respect. The disciples, like most of their fellow Jews, considered the rich to be the most respected members of the community, so if the best among them could not be saved, then there was no hope for anyone. Jesus replied by saying that salvation is impossible with human beings alone, but only possible with God. Thus the key to salvation is that one trust in God completely, and follow him wherever he goes.

In response to the failure of the rich man, Peter claimed that he and the rest of the disciples had followed Jesus completely. What reward, then, should they expect to receive? All of the synoptics record that Jesus promised that each would receive a hundredfold of blessings from God and eternal life. However, Matthew adds that at the renewal of all things (the new world) they would sit on thrones judging the twelve tribes of Israel. Some believe this is to be understood literally, but others, spiritually. If literal, then Jesus would place his disciples on thrones in his earthly kingdom to share in the rule. If spiritual, then the apostles can expect to receive special honor in heaven. However Matthew's version is to be interpreted, most likely the author included this material in his gospel because he wanted to stress that Jesus, who came to earth to establish the kingdom, was the Son of David the King. According to Matthew and Mark, Jesus concluded this saying with the memorable words, "But many who are first will be last, and the last will be first." When the kingdom comes in its fullness, there will be a reversal of order of importance—those considered important will be no greater than any other. Jesus may have included this as a rebuke of the disciples for seeking personal greatness.

Parable of the laborers in the vineyard (Matthew 20:1-16)

Matthew adds a parable to highlight the principle that the first will be last and the last first. This is a parable about an owner of a vineyard who hired workers to work his fields at various hours of the day, beginning at 6 a.m. to 5 p.m. After the day of work was over, the owner paid everyone the same amount, beginning with the ones hired last to the first ones hired. The ones who where hired first became angry because they believed that they deserved more pay than the ones who worked only one hour. The owner reminded them that they agreed to the amount and that the money was his to use as he wished.

While such employment practices might be hard to justify in today's world, the point of the parable is not about management and labor but about God's grace and the proper humble attitude his disciples should possess. The parable rebukes those who protest the opening of the kingdom to the undeserving" According to the context in Matthew, the immediate message may have been to the apostles that, although they were the first to follow Christ, they should not seek or expect special honor. All Christians are equal in the sight of God. Anyone who enters the kingdom will receive the same reward as all other Christians: salvation. Heavenly rewards are God's gifts of grace; therefore, no one should feel superior to another disciple or feel deserving of more reward.

The Ambition of James and John (Matthew 20:20-28, Mark 10:35-45)

As they were journeying to Jerusalem, Jesus gave his third and final prediction of his death and resurrection (Matthew 20:17-19, Mark 10:32-34, Luke 18:31-34). Following this, James and John requested special places of honor when Jesus assumed power in his kingdom. Matthew adds the role of the mother of James and John to this scene. The cumulative evidence from Scripture reveals that her name was Salome and possibly the sister of Mary, which would have made John and James cousins of Jesus (Matthew 27:56, Mark 15:40, John 19:25). Jesus had earlier promised all of the 12 honor, glory, and thrones, but James and John were still not satisfied.

Jesus then told them they did not know what they were asking. To be honored with Jesus, they must follow Jesus wherever he went. Jesus asked if they were willing to drink his cup and receive his baptism. In this context, the cup and baptism of Jesus was his suffering and death. In the garden of Gethsemane, Jesus asked that this cup be taken from him. James and John said they were willing to drink the cup and receive the baptism, which in fact Jesus said they would do. According to Acts 12:1-2, James was executed by Herod Agrippa in the early forties. If the John of Revelation 1:9-11 is the apostle John, then he experienced imprisonment and exile for the faith.

When the other ten disciples heard the conversation between Jesus and the sons of Zebedee, they became angry with James and John. Jesus, sensing this anger, said that most people look for greatness in exercising power and dominance, and having others serve them. The disciples of Christ, however, are to follow an opposite path. Greatness in the kingdom will be realized through service. Jesus pointed to himself as the ultimate example of service, to the point of giving his life so that others might have life.

The ministry of Jesus near or in the city of Jericho

The healing of Bartimaeus (Matthew 20:29-34, Mark 10:46-52, Luke 18:35-43)

Jesus and his band of disciples continued their journey to Jerusalem and came to Jericho. Each of the synoptic gospels records a healing of a blind man (or men) near the city. However, some slight differences between the accounts exists. According to Matthew, Jesus healed two blind men whom he met as he was leaving Jericho. Mark and Luke mention only one blind man, whom Mark named Bartimaeus. Jesus met him as he approached the city. The story describes the blind man's persistent desire to meet Jesus, the crowd's indifference, and Jesus' compassion.

Zacchaeus and Jesus (Luke 19:1-10)

Only Luke records this story of Jesus meeting the despised rich man, Zacchaeus. For Luke, this story presents a nice contrast from the previous one. The text gives the impression that after Jesus healed a poor, blind beggar, he enter the city and stay with the very wealthy tax collector. This is the sixth time that Luke mentions a tax collector, and in every case they are portrayed favorably. Since Jericho was a wealthy town, the Romans had designated it as a center for collection of taxes. Zacchaeus was the chief tax collector, which means that he had collectors who worked under him. Most likely, Zacchaeus was responsible for an entire district, a position which would have made him very rich.

As Jesus entered the city, Zacchaeus decided he wanted to see Jesus. Since he was too short to see Jesus in the crowd, he climbed a sycamore tree in order to see him. Jesus saw Zaccaeus and asked if he could stay with him. The crowd became upset because they considered Zaccaeus a sinner who had no right to be near Jesus. In contrast, Zacchaeus joyfully received Jesus into his house and declared that he would right any wrongs for which he may have been responsible and committed himself to helping the poor. For Jesus, this was a sign of true repentance. He declared that salvation had truly come to this man's house. Jesus also stated that his mission was not to go to the saved, but to the lost.

Chapter 19

Jesus in Jerusalem

According to the testimony of all four gospels, Jesus' last week of life was spent in or near Jerusalem. No other week of Jesus' life was chronicled in as much detail as this last week. Jesus' last week was filled with controversy and debates with the religious leaders, important instructions to his disciples, the last supper, and Jesus' arrest, trial, conviction, crucifixion and resurrection. If we follow the gospel of Mark, we will discover the following chronology of events of Jesus' last week:

Day One - Sunday (Palm Sunday)

- Triumphant entry
- Return to Bethany

Day Two - Monday

- Cursing of the fig tree
- Cleansing of the temple

Day Three – Tuesday

- A day of teaching and stories
- The condemnation of the religious leaders
- The Olivet discourse

Day Four - Wednesday

- Anointing at Bethany (possibly earlier)
- Judas agrees to betray Jesus

Day Five - Thursday

Passover

The Last Supper

Prayer in the garden

Arrest and night trials before Sanhedrin

Day Six - Friday

Trials before Pilate and Herod

Condemnation

Crucifixion

Burial

Day Seven - Saturday (sabbath)

Jesus in the tomb

Day Eight - Sunday

The Resurrection

There are minor differences between the gospels with regard to chronology, but they are not worthy of mention here. In this chapter, the events that occurred on days one and two will be briefly examined.

The triumphant entry of Jesus (Matthew 21:1-9, Mark 11:1-10, Luke 19:28-38)

As Jesus approached Jerusalem, Jesus sent two of his disciples with instructions to prepare for his public entrance into the city. The instructions suggest his entry was planned. Matthew indicates the plan was to follow the prophecy of Zechariah 9:9 (21:4). The use of a donkey for Jesus to ride was to be symbolic of the Messiah, envisioned by Zechariah. Since the Messiah was to be a peaceful ruler of God's kingdom, his entry into Jerusalem was an act by which he offered himself to the people as the promised Messiah. The crowd received him as a triumphant king. The cry "hosanna" originally meant "save us now." The shout of the crowd, including "hosanna," comes from Psalm 118:24-27. It was originally a cry of help for deliverance. Perhaps the crowd was crying out to Jesus for deliverance or that the term, over time, had been reduced to a simple expression of praise.

The cursing of the fig tree (Matthew 21:18-22, Mark 11:12-14,20-24)

Introduction

Mark 11:11 indicates that after Jesus had spent some time in the temple area he left the city and stayed in Bethany that evening. In fact, Mark suggests that Jesus' practice was to spend the night in Bethany after each day's activities in Jerusalem. The next morning, Mark states as Jesus and his disciples were traveling to Jerusalem they came upon a fig tree, which he cursed for having no fruit. Then he proceeded to the city where he entered the temple and cleansed the temple of the money changers and sellers of animals for sacrifice. Whatever the cursing of the fig tree and the cleansing of the temple meant, Mark intends for the reader to see the two events as related--that the cursing of the fig tree somehow prefigured the cleansing of the temple. Matthew also understands the fig tree episode as symbolic of God's judgment on Jerusalem, including the temple, but he describes the cleansing of the temple as if it took place the day before the cursing of the fig tree.

The strange miracle

The cursing of the fig tree is the only miracle of Jesus which was purely destructive. Mark points out that there were no figs on the tree, and it was not yet the time for figs. When Jesus saw that there was nothing edible on the tree, he cursed it. Matthew seems to indicate that the tree withered immediately, while Mark indicates that the disciples noticed the withered tree on the following day.

The significance of the miracle

For Mark, the cleansing of the temple immediately followed this event. Possibly Mark understood this miracle as primarily an event by which Jesus acted out a parable by means of a miracle in order to point out that Jerusalem, or even Israel, would come under divine judgment, even as that fruitless fig tree. Both Matthew and Mark also emphasize that this miracle demonstrated the power of genuine faith in God; there are no boundaries to what is possible.

The cleansing of the temple (Matthew 21:10-17, Mark 11:15-19, Luke 19:19-45-48)

Introduction

No other event in the life of Jesus did more to guarantee his death than when he cleansed the temple. As the cursing of the fig tree was the only miracle where Jesus destroyed something, the cleansing of the temple is the only event where Jesus used some measure of violence. The event itself is rather simple to describe. Jesus entered the temple and drove out the money changers and sellers of doves, overturned their tables and prevented people from taking their merchandise or money out of the temple. Then Jesus said that God's house shall be called a house of prayer and not a den of thieves. What is less clear is why Jesus did this, and what was it that was so objectionable about buying and selling in the temple area? Lastly, what was it that Jesus wanted to accomplish by his actions?

The problem with buying and selling in the temple

During religious holidays like Passover, thousands of people would travel to Jerusalem for worship. If someone had traveled a long distance, did not own sheep, or was poor, most likely that person would enter Jerusalem without a lamb or dove to offer to God, so those who could afford it would buy the appropriate sacrificial animal from the temple merchants and offer it to God. Usually, the merchants would charge inflated prices for these animals. In addition, the temple merchants would only accept temple currency, which meant that would-be buyers would have to exchange their money for temple currency at an exorbitant rate. Worse than that, scholars believe that sometimes the temple officials would reject a worshiper's animal for sacrifice as if it had some kind of blemish. This would force the worshiper to purchase an acceptable animal for sacrifice from the temple merchants. It appears that the temple merchants were unfairly and dishonestly exploiting the people. As Jesus would say, the temple was truly a den of thieves.

But more than exploitation of the people, this commercial activity was a desecration of the house of worship. Jesus said, "My house shall be called a house of prayer." This suggests that a place of worship is not to be a place of merchandising. Mark adds the next line from the passage in Isaiah 56:7, which says "for all the nations." According to Mark, Jesus was critical of the exclusive and isolationist policies surrounding the temple. Possibly Jesus was also upset that the money changers had taken up shop in the court of the Gentiles, thus making it harder for Gentiles to come and worship.

Jesus' reasons for cleansing the temple

Part of Jesus' reason for cleansing the temple was to make a clear and unmistakable protest against the abuse and corruption which was present in the temple. The people needed to return to the idea and practice of the temple as a place of worship with God at the center of life. Jesus may have wanted to call the ones in charge of the temple, who had at least allowed the abuse to continue, to repent and rededicate themselves as servants of God. However, he also may have understood this event as not simply prophetic, but messianic. The Old Testament prophet Malachi prophesied the coming of the Lord to the temple.

> See, I am sending my messenger to prepare the way before me, and the Lord whom you seek will suddenly come to his temple. The messenger of the covenant in whom you delight—indeed, he is coming, says the Lord of hosts. But who can endure the day of his coming, and who can stand when he appears? For he is like a refiner's fire and like fullers' soap; he will sit as a refiner and purifier of silver, and he will purify the descendants of Levi and refine them like gold and silver, until they present offerings to the Lord in righteousness. Then the offering of Judah and Jerusalem will be pleasing to the Lord as in the days of old and as in former years (Malachi 3:1-4).

Jesus may have understood himself to be the Lord's representative who would appear in the temple in judgment and renewal. However, instead of motivating the leadership to repentance, this action by Jesus led the Jewish leaders to plan a way to kill him.

Parables and questions (Matthew 21:23-22:46, Mark 11:27-12:37a, Luke 20:1-44)

The cleansing of the temple and the teaching ministry of Jesus had caused such a stir in Jerusalem that the religious leaders asked him to explain the source of his authority for doing these things. First, Jesus asked them to tell him if the baptism of John the Baptist came from God or man. The leaders saw the trap. If they said the baptism came from men, then they lost the support of the people, who revered John. If they said that the baptism came from God, then Jesus would ask them why they did not support John. So they said they did not know, and since they would not answer, Jesus would not give them an answer. (Matthew 21:23-27, Mark 11:27-33, Luke 20:1-8). Jesus further responded to their criticism by telling parables concerning the unfaithfulness of the religious leaders.

The parable of the two sons (Matthew 21:28-32)

Mark states that in response to the criticisms of the religious leaders, Jesus began to speak in parables, though he only recorded one parable in the section. Matthew though has preserved two other parables, the parable of the two sons and the parable of the wedding banquet. The parable of the two sons opens with a father summoning his children to work in the family vineyard. When summoned by the father, the first son said he would not work the vineyard, but then later changed his mind and went and worked. The other son who said he would go and work, never did. Jesus' point is that though some people rebelled against God and sinned many repented of their sins through the preaching of John. In this parable, Jesus accused the Jewish leaders, who claimed to be doing God's will, of not having repented. Yet God only accepts those who know they need God, repent of sins, and then obey his will. Those who only claim to be righteous and do not live righteously will not receive any blessing from God.

The parable of the wicked tenants (Matthew 21:33-46, Mark 12:1-12, Luke 20:9-19)

According to Matthew, Jesus told this parable immediately after the parable of the two sons. This parable is very similar to an allegory, since one can find symbolic significance for many elements in the story. For example, the vineyard represents Israel, the householder or owner of the vineyard is God, the tenants are most likely the religious leaders, the servants of the householders are the prophets, and the son of the household is Jesus. In this parable, Jesus taught that God placed into everyone's hands the responsibility for caring for his people. Throughout the years God sent numerous warnings and pleas for repentance by the mouths of the prophets, but they were always ignored or rejected. The sending of God's son is God's last warning to the religious leaders. If they reject and kill him, they would throw away their last opportunity to escape divine judgment. Like the wicked tenants, the religious leaders were guilty of being irresponsible, ambitious, and selfish and are accountable to God for their unfaithfulness.

And then, as if the Jewish authorities did not understand the parable, Jesus referred to himself as the rejected stone which had become the cornerstone. A cornerstone was the keystone upon which an entire structure was built. Jesus quoted a passage in Psalm 118:22-23, in which Israel as a nation was described as the cornerstone, and applied it to himself. Therefore, if the Jewish leaders rejected Jesus, they would be rejecting the very foundation of God's kingdom. On a different note, Matthew recorded that Jesus said that the kingdom was to be taken away from them and given to a people that would produce fruit for God. Presumably, this meant that the Jewish leaders were to be excluded from the kingdom because of their unbelief and that Gentiles were to be invited into the kingdom.

The parable of the wedding banquet (Matthew 22:1-14)

This parable in Matthew is very simila r to one in Luke 14:16-24. According to the parable, invitations were given to people to attend the wedding banquet of the son of the king. However, when the banquet was ready to begin, the guests gave many different excuses for not attending the banquet. Some even mistreated, beat, and killed the messengers of the king. The king in his anger ordered his troops to the city. They attacked, killed those who murdered the king's servants, and burned their city. After his anger had dissipated, the king decided that more invitations be extended to anyone whom they found, and by this method they filled the banquet hall.

However, when the king arrived at the banquet, he saw that one of the guests was not wearing a wedding robe. His inappropriate dress showed either a lack of understanding or a refusal to wear the proper attire. Some people believe that the last part of the parable is really a separate parable that was later attached to this one. I will treat this passage as one parable. When the king approached the man, he asked the man why he was dressed inappropriately. The man had no answer. Therefore, the king ordered that the man be thrown out of the banquet, bound and gagged, and sent into the outer darkness (i.e., hell). The garments probably stand for righteousness. Thus, the meaning of the parable is that one must not only respond to the call of the gospel, but he must also put on righteousness.

Questions concerning taxes (Matthew 22:15-22, Mark 12:13-17, Luke 20:20-36)

The gospel story shifts from Jesus' strong criticism of the religious leaders by means of parable to questions that were asked of Jesus in order to trap and discredit him. Matthew and Mark record three questions that were posed to Jesus. Luke has only two, although he presented a similar version of Mark and Matthew's question concerning the greatest commandment in his dialogue with a lawyer (Luke 10:25-28). The first question that was asked of Jesus was whether or not one should pay taxes. This was clearly a loaded question. If Jesus answered that everyone, including Jews, should pay taxes, then the Jewish crowd would have turned against him, since they hated Rome. However, if he were to say that they should not pay taxes, then Rome would see him as a troublemaker and rabble rouser.

Jesus responded by asking to see a coin, a denarius. He asked whose image was on the coin. It was Caesar's. Jesus then told them to give back to the emperor what belonged to him, i.e. taxes. His primary concern was that people give themselves to God in faith and obedience.

A question concerning the resurrection (Matthew 22:23-33, Mark 12:18-27, Luke 20:27-40)

The Sadducees, who did not believe in resurrection, posed the question based on the Mosaic statute concerning the so-called Levirate marriage (Deuteronomy 25:5-10). The Levirate marriage statute states that if a man dies and leaves a wife without fathering any children by her the next of kin is supposed to marry her and father a child in the name of the deceased brother or next of kin. This question concerns a woman whose husband died leaving no children. She then married (one at a time) each of the six remaining brothers, all of whom also died without fathering any children. So at the resurrection, whose wife would she be? Women in first century marriages were regarded, at best, to be second-class citizens, and at worst, little more than property. The question was not about the perpetuating of a marriage relationship, but of male power and ownership.

Jesus responded that their question revealed two major flaws with their thinking. They were ignorant of the Scripture in Exodus (one of the books the Sadducees highly revered) where God told Moses that he was the God of Abraham, Isaac, and Jacob. God is the God of the living and not the dead. If God is the God of the living, all the dead who were faithful are still alive in some way. Secondly, the Sadducees were ignorant of the power of God. Life after the resurrection will be completely different. Eternal life is more than a simple never-ending existence, but life on a whole different plane of existence with God. Relationships will be completely different based on a wholly different standard. Perhaps Jesus said there would be no marriages in heaven as a way of saying that there would be complete equality among everyone, and that no one will own or control another.

A question concerning the law (Matthew 22:34-40, Mark 12:28-34)

This question concerning the law was posed by a Pharisee, whom Mark described as a scribe. There are 613 statutes in the Mosaic Law. It appears that the scribe's question was concerned with which of these was the most important. Jesus' response focused more on the principle of Law. Jesus said that the commandment to love God is the greatest commandment, and the one about loving one's neighbor the next greatest commandment. Then he said that all the law and the prophets, the entirety of the Jewish faith, are based on these two commandments. The person who truly loves God will be obedient to God's word and the prompting of the Spirit. The person who truly loves his or her neighbor will always seek to live a life of compassion and integrity before others. Love, therefore, is the greatest commandment because the whole law is summed up in this one law.

Jesus' unanswerable question about David's descendant (Matthew 22:41-46, Mark 12:35-37a, Luke 20:41-44)

After Jesus had responded to his critics' loaded questions, he then asked them a question, for which none of his hearers had an answer. Based on Psalm 110:1, Jesus asked how David, the author of the psalm, could speak of his descendant as Lord. If David spoke of his descendant as Lord, he was in fact affirming his descendant's superiority to him. How could David speak this way? Jesus may have asked this primarily to silence his critics by forcing them to contemplate the meaning of the psalm.

Jesus' warning against the scribes and pharisees (Matthew 23:1-39, Mark 12:37b-40, Luke 20:45-47)

Turning then to the crowds who had been observing his dialogue with the religious leaders, Jesus proceeded to warn them of the religious hypocrisy and arrogance of the religious leaders. Matthew 23 contains a much longer discourse of condemnation against the Pharisees and scribes. In Matthew's version, Jesus repeatedly pronounced the prophetic "woe" upon the leaders.

The "woe" was a type of public condemnation expressed like a lamentation. The thrust of the woes was that the Pharisees had misused, twisted, and expanded the law of Moses through their traditions, so that serving God became a burden which no one, not even the Pharisees, could bear. All of the synoptics record that Jesus condemned the scribes and Pharisees for their pride and ostentation. Jesus accused them of oppressing the poor, particularly widows, for personal gain. Even religious acts, including prayer and giving alms, were done by the religious leaders simply or primarily for public approval. Despite all their claims of righteousness, these religious leaders stood under God's condemnation.

The widow's offering (Mark 12:41-44, Luke 21:1-4)

An illustration of the Pharisees' hypocrisy is highlighted in the story of the widow's offering. According to Mark and Luke, money was being collected in the temple precincts to help support the temple service and provide relief for the poor. While the rich (no doubt including Pharisees and Sadducees) gave a great deal, Jesus identified the widow's small gift of two copper coins that Jesus identified as the greatest gift. This widow may very well have given all of her monetary possessions, while the rich gave out of their abundance. Moreover, there must have been some public demonstration of the offerings by the rich. Jesus made it clear that God is interested in the heart of the giver. Real giving is not about the amount of the gift but about the attitude with which it is given.

Chapter 20

The Olivet Discourse
(Matthew 24-25, Mark 13, Luke 21)

Introduction

The last major discourse of Jesus recorded in the gospels is often called the Olivet Discourse. Matthew, Mark, and Luke record a lengthy discourse Jesus gave concerning the destruction of Jerusalem and the final judgment of the world. Matthew and Mark state that Jesus said these words to his disciples on the Mount of Olives. The structure of the discourse is about the same in all three gospels, except that Matthew's is much longer because he included three parables and a final judgment scene. One major difference between the three versions is that in Mark and Luke the disciples asked Jesus, "When will Jerusalem and the temple be destroyed?" but in Matthew they asked "When will Jerusalem be destroyed and what will be the sign of Jesus' second coming and the end of the age?" For Matthew, this is the last of the five great discourses of Jesus in this gospel, though some believe the discourse actually begins in chapter 23. Due to the wealth of material in Matthew's version, this study will focus on the Olivet Discourse according to Matthew.

Jesus' prediction and the disciples' question

The context for Jesus' discourse in Matthew is his words at the end of chapter 23 where he laments over the demise of Jerusalem (23:37). He then made this ominous observation and prediction: "See, your house is left to you, desolate. For I tell you, you will not see me again until you say, 'Blessed is the one who comes in the name of the Lord'" (23:38-39). Jesus had declared that God had abandoned them, that he was no longer present in the temple. With the absence of God, Jerusalem was completely vulnerable to attack by anyone. He then said that they would not see him again until they recognized and confessed him to be the king, which he implied would only happen on the Judgment Day. Having declared Jerusalem and the temple with the religious leaders to be under divine judgment, Jesus left the temple area. Matthew states that his disciples began to point out to him the various buildings in the temple complex. According to Mark, the disciples had been struck with awe at the impressive size of the buildings. However, Luke mentions that some people, now specifically called disciples, were impressed with the beauty of the temple. In response to this, Jesus declared that the very stones which made up the temple would be thrown down. The temple was going to be destroyed. When Jesus and the disciples reached the Mount of Olives, the disciples asked him when that would happen. Matthew words the disciples' question this way: "Tell us, when will this be, and what will be the sign of your coming and of the end of the age?" (Matthew 24:3b).

According to Matthew, the disciples asked two questions or one question with two parts. The first had to do with the destruction of Jerusalem and the temple. The second was concerned with the second coming of Jesus at the close of the age. It may be that the disciples actually had only one question, as Mark and Luke record, but that they believed the destruction of Jerusalem meant the end of the world. Jesus' response to the disciples' questions may be divided into four parts: (1) Instructions concerning the destruction of Jerusalem (24:4-28); (2) Instruction concerning the coming of the Son of Man (24:29-35); (3) An exhortation to watchfulness in preparation for the coming of the Son of Man (24:36-25:30; (4) The Great Judgment (25:31-46).

Instructions concerning the destruction of Jerusalem (Matthew 24:4-28)

Jesus' words begin with a warning to the disciples against those who would deceive them. They must not allow themselves to be led astray by others who claim that certain events signal the return of the messiah to his people. There will be false messiahs and horrible calamities which seem to point to the nearness of the end. Yet the rise in war and natural disasters do not necessarily mean the end is near. He described these events as "the beginning of the birth pangs." Jesus also pointed out that even the rise of apostasy, false teachers and prophets, persecution of Christians, and a general moral and spiritual disintegration of society does not the mean the end of the world. These will be times when God's people will be called to practice a high degree of faithfulness in the midst of spiritual darkness. Moreover, the Church must proclaim the gospel to this dying world. Only after the world has had the opportunity to hear the gospel will the end come, but until that day comes, Christians must be faithful.

The most dreadful event Jews and Jewish Christians had to face was the destruction of Jerusalem and the temple. The thought of Jerusalem's demise most likely would have brought about thoughts of the end of the world. For Jesus, the destruction was a symbol and precursor to the end, but it was not the end itself. According to Matthew and Mark, Jesus described the events that were to happen as "the desolating sacrilege." The expression "the desolating sacrilege" refers to Daniel's prophecy concerning the desecration of the temple by Antiochus IV, which sparked the Maccabean Revolt (Daniel 9:27, 11:31, 12:11). The desecration which Jesus predicted was the temple's actual destruction. When these events begin to occur, Jesus said those in Judea should immediately flee to the mountains. Jesus said that these future events would be absolutely horrific, the worst in human history, and that only by the mercy of God will any of his people survive. Nevertheless, it would not mean that Jesus had come. There would still be false claims of messiahs and false prophets performing miracles in order to lead some of the chosen people astray, so the disciples must not be deceived. When the Son of Man comes there will be no doubt about it. His coming will be as self-evident as flashes of lightning across the sky. His coming will also be as inevitable as vultures around a corpse.

Instructions concerning the coming of the Son of Man (Matthew 24:28-35)

The coming of the Son of Man is described as an event of cosmic significance. With the use of symbols, Jesus described his coming to be cataclysmic, with power and glory, causing fear within humanity since judgment day has come. One difficulty is that according to Matthew the coming of the Son of Man will take place "immediately after the suffering of those days" (Matthew 24:29). How should one interpret the word "immediately?" If Jesus meant that the second coming was to happen soon after the destruction of Jerusalem, then he was mistaken. Some people believe that the suffering described in Matthew 24:9-28 is not the destruction of Jerusalem but a suffering to take place sometime in the future. The suffering would last for about seven years. Then immediately after that Jesus would return to judge the wicked and establish an earthly kingdom that would last for one thousand years. However, Jesus only spoke of his coming to judge and not of any thousand-year earthly rule. Mark and Luke do not have the word "immediately." Another interpretation is that "immediately" should be translated as "suddenly." The emphasis would not be on the time of Jesus' coming, but on the nature of it.

Jesus used the example of the fig tree to point out that future events will be preceded by signs. Some have suggested Jesus was referring to the events that preceded the destruction of Jerusalem. However, the context in Matthew would indicate that Jesus was saying that his coming would be preceded by certain signs. Perhaps Jesus saw some kind of analogy between the destruction of Jerusalem and the coming of the Son of Man. As the destruction of Jerusalem was preceded by suffering and war, in a similar way the coming of the Son of Man will be preceded by a period of suffering and persecution. He then mentioned that "this generation will not pass away until all these things have taken place" (Matthew 24:34, Mark 13:30, Luke 21:32). Who is this generation that will not pass away? And what things have to take place? This is very difficult to interpret. If "this generation" means the generation of the first disciples of Jesus, then the "things" must be the destruction of Jerusalem. However, if "this generation" refers to the human race, then it means that humanity will endure until everything God has planned takes place.

An exhortation for watchfulness in preparation for the coming of the Son of Man (Matthew 24:35-25:30)

The coming of the Son of Man will be sudden and unexpected. He will come at a time similar to the days of Noah--a time when people going about the normal daily activities of life have no awareness of what was about to happen. Moreover, the Son of Man's coming will be a time of separation and judgment, of great calamity and disaster, and there will be no escape. Therefore, Jesus exhorted them to keep on the alert and be prepared for the Lord's return. As a homeowner cannot predict when a thief will break into his house, so the disciples do not know when Jesus will return. Consequently, like the homeowner who simply prepares his house for the break in, followers must prepare themselves for the Lord's return.

Parable of the faithful and wise slave

With this in mind, Jesus told a parable about a faithful and unfaithful servant. What Jesus actually said seems to be the summary/application of a parable. The parable may have been like this:

> Suppose there was a certain master who entrusted a servant with the management of the entire household. If that servant carried out his responsibilities with great diligence, including caring for the rest of the master's servants, he will be rewarded when the master unexpectedly returns. Truly that master will praise that servant and promote him to a position of honor above his fellow servants, but if that same servant had chosen instead to act in a selfish, irresponsible, and even abusive way, the master upon return will certainly punish him severely.

The lesson of the parable is that the disciples must be watchful and alert in their spiritual and moral lives. The foolish and dangerous thing is to assume that Jesus is gone for a long time and that one has plenty of time to do what is right. Since the parable had to do with servants who had positions of authority in the master's household, this parable may also be about the serious responsibility of being a leader among God's people.

Parable of the ten bridesmaids (Matthew 25:1-13)

Matthew adds two parables which call for faithfulness until Jesus returns. The first parable is about ten bridesmaids who serve at a wedding. The setting of the parable is the period of waiting for the arrival of the bridegroom for his bride. On this occasion, the bridegroom is late. As the hour grew very late, the bridesmaids fell asleep. At midnight the bridegroom arrived to a sleeping wedding party to claim his bride. When they awoke, five of the ten bridesmaids discovered that they had run out of oil for their lamps. Since it was not possible for the other five to share their oil with those who needed oil, these five went to purchase additional oil. After purchasing the oil, they returned, only to find that the wedding feast had already begun without them, and the doors were closed. They pleaded for the master to let them in, but he refused, claiming he did not know them. The point of the parable is that disciples must be faithful for the duration. If we are not prepared to be faithful for as long as it takes, we risk missing out on the blessings of the kingdom.

Parable of the talents (Matthew 25:14-30)

The second parable Matthew records is about a businessman who entrusted three of his servants with a certain amount of money. This businessman gave five talents to one servant, two to another, and one to still another. The rich man then left for a long time. Upon his return, he summoned his three servants to find out how well they had invested the funds he had entrusted to them. Both the five and two talent servants had doubled the amount they had invested. Because of their good work, the master praised and rewarded them. However, the servant who had been given one talent had hid his talent because he was afraid of losing it. The master became angry at the one talent servant. He ordered the one talent to be given to the servant with ten, and the unproductive servant to be dismissed and possibly thrown into jail. Through this parable, Jesus taught that God expects each disciple to responsibly use the blessings God has given him or her and to take advantage of every opportunity to do good. There is more to life than survival. One must be willing to step out in faith. This is what is meant by faithfulness until Jesus returns.

The Great Judgment (Matthew 25:31-46)

The final saying in Matthew's Olivet Discourse is a depiction of the Final Judgment. Jesus said that on the day of judgment there will be a great separation of humanity. As with many of Jesus' teachings, people are divided into two groups, the sheep and the goats. Earlier Matthew spoke of the wheat and weeds, the wise and foolish builders, the wise and foolish bridesmaids, and the faithful and unfaithful servants. In his teachings, the Son of Man, Jesus, separates people for eternal blessing or punishment. The standard of judgment seems to be one's response to human need. Some scholars, however, have suggested that the people designated "one of the least of these who are members of my family" means only fellow disciples of Jesus.The faithful gave assistance without any thought of divine blessing or that God was aware of the actions. Moreover, the faithful learned that by ministering to the various people, they were actually ministering to the Lord. Those who were under condemnation said that they were not aware that the Lord had been among them or else they would have cared for him. Jesus responded that their failure to serve others in need means that they failed to serve Jesus. However this parable is interpreted, clearly God is calling Christians to be people of compassion.

Chapter 21

Preparing for the Cross

The Anointing of Jesus (Matthew 26:6-13, Mark 14:3-9)

Introduction

All four gospels record an event wherein Jesus is anointed by a woman. Luke records an anointing which took place early in Jesus' ministry at the house of Simon the Pharisee. However, it is not likely that that episode in Jesus' life is the same one described in Matthew and Mark. The Gospel of John records the same anointing of Jesus as in Matthew and Mark but places it before the triumphal entry; six days before Passover (John 12:1-11), while Matthew and Mark place it after the triumphal entry. An interesting note is that Matthew and Mark place the anointing of Jesus just before or after the decision by Judas Iscariot to betray Jesus, as if to show a contrast between the kindness and faith of the woman and the betrayal of one of his own disciples. While people are seeking to kill Jesus, a woman is preparing his body for burial. Furthermore, the anointing story in John 12:1-11, though the same story as in Matthew and Mark, is told much differently. For example, John said that a woman named Mary anointed Jesus' feet, but in Matthew and Mark, the woman anointed Jesus' head.

Rather than trying to explain these and other differences, we will examine only the account in Matthew and Mark.

The Anointing

According to Matthew and Mark, this event took place at the house of Simon the Leper during dinner. Matthew and Mark record that an unnamed woman anointed Jesus with nard, which was an expensive perfume extracted from a root in India. The flask was sealed until used. The neck of the flask had to be broken in order to open it. Matthew and Mark said that she anointed Jesus' head, through which she may have honored Jesus as a king or the Messiah.

The disciples were disturbed at the waste associated with the anointing. The money the perfume was worth could have been given to the poor, as it was customary to give to the poor at Passover time. Jesus defended the woman and stated that the poor will always exist. Further, the needs of Jesus, whom they will not always have, were more important or took precedent over some traditional practice. Beyond all that, Jesus recognized and declared that, in reality, this had been preparing his body for burial. So her act was a prelude to his death. As a result, Jesus promised that her act of kindness would always be remembered.

The plot to destroy Jesus (Matthew 26:1-5, 14-16, Mark 14:1-2, 10-11, Luke 22:1-6)

As a result of all that Jesus had said and taught, the Jewish leaders decided that Jesus must die. Previously, Jesus had repeatedly told the disciples that his death was to take place during Passover. Why did the Chief Priest and elders want to kill Jesus? First, Jesus had been hailed as king by the people at the triumphal entry. When Jesus cleansed the temple, the people saw him as a reformer, and the leaders saw him as a threat to their institution and positions. Jesus' devastating criticism of the religious leaders just before this made him an even greater threat. Some may have feared that because of his influence the people might revolt against Rome. Others may have feared he was a blasphemer who could lead others away from the Law. In order to avoid publicity, the leaders decided on a secret arrest and trial so that the people might not revolt, but in order to successfully arrest Jesus, someone would have to get the soldiers close to Jesus. Judas would be the one who would help them secretly arrest him.

The text indicates that Judas took the initiative by approaching the priests with his proposal. Judas' fee for helping the priests arrest Jesus was 30 pieces of silver, the common price for a slave. One of the great mysteries of biblical study is determining a motive behind Judas' betrayal. One of the oldest theories is that Judas was driven by greed. His plan may have been to take the money and escape with his life. If money was the motivation, he certainly did not seek a very high reward for services rendered. A second theory speculates that Judas was overcome by hatred and disillusionment. He may have come to disbelieve in Jesus and saw him as dangerous. He gave up faith in Jesus when he realized that Jesus had no intention to drive out the Romans by military force. Perhaps the least likely interpretation is that Judas betrayed Jesus to force him to assert and defend himself as Messiah. He may have thought Jesus would use his power when forced to. However, when Jesus refused to use his power, even to defend himself, Judas was personally and emotionally shattered.

The Last Supper

Introduction

One of the most sacred traditions in the Christian religion is the Lord's Supper--also called Communion or the Eucharist. Since the beginning of the Church, Christians have observed this sacred rite as part of their corporate worship. Evidence both from the New Testament books of Acts and 1 Corinthians, as well as writings from the early church fathers, indicate that Communion was originally observed in house churches as part of a fellowship meal. In addition to commemorating the death of Jesus, early Christians partook of the meal to celebrate the invisible presence of the living Jesus and to reaffirm their fellowship as brothers and sisters joined together by faith in Jesus. In later years, the Church limited Communion observance to the two elements of bread and wine. The origin for the Lord's Supper is the meal Jesus shared with his disciples.

Since that meal was most likely a Passover meal, it is necessary to present some background information concerning Passover observance in order to show that Jesus' last supper was very consistent with a Passover meal.

Passover preparation (Matthew 17-19, Mark 14:12-16, Luke 22:7-13)

Jesus instructed his disciples how to prepare for the special evening meal. He told them they would see a man carrying a water jar, an unusual sight since normally women carried the jars. Jesus' instructions appear to indicate that previous secret arrangements had been made with someone secretly in order to avoid suspicion. Every indication is that the last supper Jesus ate with his disciples was the Passover meal. In order to better understand what took place, it is appropriate to outline the general procedures for Passover preparation. Two festivals, Passover and Unleavened Bread, are mentioned in the gospels. Passover was a one day festival, with the evening meal usually eaten after sundown. The second festival was Unleavened Bread, which was a seven day festival which immediately followed Passover.

On the morning before Passover celebration, every family would carefully search their house to find and remove all leaven. No leaven was to be found in the house. In preparation for the meal, unleavened bread was made. A lamb was roasted, originally over an open fire on a spit. As the time drew near for the meal, the following table items were set: *(1) a bowl of salt water; (2) a collection of bitter herbs, which includes horseradish, chicory, endive, parsley, lettuce; (3) a paste or relish called "charosheth," made of apples, dates, pomegranates, nuts with sticks of cinnamon; and (4) four cups of wine.*

The Passover Meal

Accurate information concerning the actual practice of Passover in the first century is scarce. However, the following description of the first-century Jewish ritual of Passover is reliable concerning the major elements of the sacred rite. The supper began with a ceremonial **first cup of wine called the "Kiddush,"** which means consecration. Usually the leader of the Passover, would introduce the **evening and offer prayers**. The **first ceremonial cleansing of hands** followed the opening prayers. Once the celebrants had **ceremonially washed their hands,** they would proceed with the eating of the **bitter herbs dipped in salt water.** This act was intended to commemorate the bitter tears of slavery during Israel's bondage. Then came the first breaking of bread in memory of the bondage in Egypt.

At this point in the ceremony, the **father or male leader of the meal explained the meaning of Passover to the son or some younger male attendee.** First, the son asked the questions concerning Passover. The father then answered the son by quoting Deuteronomy 26:5-15, which retells the story of the exodus of Israel from Egypt to become the people of God. In grateful response, the son responded by quoting the Hallel, Psalm 113-118 (or parts of it).

With the conclusion of the explanation part of the ritual, **the second cup of wine** was consumed, followed by the **second ceremonial hand washing.** Then **grace** was offered for the **main meal**, after which more bitter herbs were eaten with some placed between two pieces of Passover bread dipped in the charosheth. At this point the main meal of Passover was eaten. In accordance with the Mosaic Law, everything had to be eaten. After people had finished eating, the group spent a **period of time in thanksgiving through songs and the recitation of scripture.** Then there was a **third cup of wine, which was known as the cup of thanksgiving or redemption**, followed by a **prayer.** As the meal came to an end, **a fourth cup of wine was drunk**, after which there **was singing of the psalms from the Hallel, especially Psalm 113,** the Great Hallel. Then there were two final **closing prayers and a concluding shout of praise**.

The Last Supper as a Passover meal

With this understanding of first-century Jewish Passover practice, it is possible to interpret the gospel's description of the Last Supper in light of Passover. First, Luke 22:17 says Jesus took a cup before the bread and the meal. This may have been the "Kiddush," the first cup of consecration. Then as they were eating (most likely the meal proper), Jesus predicted that the betrayer would be the one who dipped in the dish (the charosheth) with him (Matthew 26:21-23, Mark 14:18-20). Also, during the meal,

Jesus took bread, blessed it, broke it, and said it was his body given for them (Matthew 26:26, Mark 14:22). Luke 22:20 states Jesus took the cup after supper, gave thanks, gave it to them, and told them it was his blood poured for many for the forgiveness of sin (Matthew 26:28, Mark 14:23-24). This may have been the third cup of Passover--the cup of redemption. Matthew 26:30 and Mark 14:26 mention that they concluded the evening by singing the hymn, most likely the Great Hallel. Some scholars have argued that the absence of any reference to the Passover lamb is either evidence that Jesus was not celebrating Passover or that he removed the lamb from the meal since he was the true lamb of God. However, it is more likely the lamb was not mentioned because it was not important for the writer to mention it. What is important is that Jesus asked the disciples to remember him whenever they broke bread and drank wine together.

Jesus in the garden (Matthew 26:36-46, Mark 14:32-42, Luke 22:40-46)

With the conclusion of the meal, Jesus went to the garden of Gethsemane, which is located on the Mount of Olives. The Mount of Olives was east of Jerusalem across the Kidron Valley. Most likely, Gethsemane was a private olive orchard. According to John, this was a favorite meeting spot for Jesus and his disciples. When Jesus came to the entrance of the garden, he took Peter, James, and John further into the garden but left the remaining nine at the entrance. Jesus then went alone even further to pray by himself. Matthew and Mark describe Jesus in prayer as one extremely troubled about what was soon going to happen. In some ancient manuscripts, Luke describes Jesus as being in such anguish that his sweat appeared like big drops of blood as it fell to the ground. This text says that he prayed for one hour, in which he asked that this cup, his suffering and death on the cross, might be taken away from him. But also he accepted God's will, whatever it would be. Jesus returned to find his three closest disciples sleeping, so he prayed a second hour, again accepting the Father's will. He returned and found the disciples still asleep. Then he prayed a third hour, praying essentially the same thing and again accepting the decision of the Father concerning his prayer.

Chapter 22

The Arrest and Trial of Jesus

The betrayal and arrest (Matthew 26:47-56, Mark 14:43-52, Luke 22:47-53)

When Jesus entered Jerusalem, he knew that he was entering a dangerous place. Several times before his arrest Jesus had told his disciples that suffering and death awaited him in Jerusalem, yet he still went there. His words at the Supper, where he pointed to the bread and wine as symbolic of his body and blood, was a clear indication that Jesus expected his life to end in a short while. The portrayal of Jesus in prayer in the garden showed that while he did not want to drink this cup of suffering he realized it was the heavenly Father's will. So, when Judas led a large company of people, many armed with weapons, to arrest Jesus and charge him with heresy, Jesus was not surprised. Nevertheless, he must have been hurt that one of the twelve had been responsible for his arrest.

The text states that Judas betrayed Jesus with a kiss. In ancient times, such a kiss would normally be described as an expression of friendship. Yet, Judas apparently kissed Jesus in order to point him out. Perhaps it was so dark that Jesus would not be easily identifiable or some of the people who came to arrest him had never seen him close up or in person.

Then in a courageous yet foolish attempt to defend Jesus, one of the disciples drew a sword, presumably to engage in battle, and cut off the ear of the slave of the high priest. John identifies Jesus' would-be defender as Peter and the injured slave as Malchus (18:10-11). Jesus, however, rebuked the disciple. Luke then adds he healed the man's ear.

After this, Jesus turned to his captors and accused them of cowardice because they arrested him secretly at night and not during the day when he was publicly teaching. He suggested that their actions were excessive, treating him like a common thief. Nevertheless, Jesus submitted to their arrest since he viewed it as a fulfillment to Scripture. At this point, Matthew and Mark indicate that the disciples all deserted him and fled. Mark adds there was a young man wearing only a linen cloth who fled from the arrest scene naked when the group attempted to seize him. While no one knows who this young man was, some have suggested that it was Mark himself.

The trial of Jesus

The gospels record that Jesus endured several hearings, both official and unofficial, perhaps both formal and informal. Generally, scholars refer to two primary phases of the trial experience of Jesus: the Jewish phase and the Roman phase. The Jewish phase consists of the following hearings:

1. **The hearing before Annas**. This was most likely an unofficial and perhaps informal hearing before the former high priest, the father-in-law of the high priest Caiaphas. Jesus was brought there late at night, immediately following his arrest in the garden. This is found only in John 18:13-24.
2. **The night trial before the Sanhedrin**. This was an unofficial but formal hearing or trial before this Jewish court, with Caiaphas the high priest presiding. After the hearing before Annas, Jesus was brought before the Sanhedrin, in which testimony was heard by so-called witnesses, and Jesus himself was questioned. According to Matthew and Mark this happened late at night.
3. **The official and formal convening of the Sanhedrin**. At this meeting, formal charges and a verdict were delivered. This occurred

early in the Friday morning after the previous night's trials. Because their verdict of blasphemy required the death penalty, the court decided to refer Jesus to the Roman governor, Pontius Pilate.

The Roman phase of Jesus' trial can be similarly outlined:

1. **The first hearing before Pilate**. Jesus was presented to Pilate as a person who had been condemned by the Jewish court as a blasphemer and political rebel. After a brief interrogation, Pilate learned that Jesus was from Galilee, the province of Herod Antipas, so he transferred Jesus to Herod for questioning.
2. **Hearing before Herod Antipas**. While Herod was interested in meeting Jesus, he found nothing deserving death and sent him back to Pilate for final judgment.
3. **Second hearing before Pilate**. At this hearing, Jesus was formally condemned to death.

The unofficial yet formal hearing/trial before Caiaphas and the Sanhedrin (Matthew 26:57-75, Mark 14:53-72, Luke 22:54-71)

Matthew and Mark report that chief priests and the whole council had been looking for testimony that could be presented against Jesus in order to convict him. Eventually certain witnesses (Matthew says there were two), whom the gospel writers described as "false," came forward to testify against Jesus. They accused him of attacking the temple and possibly its worship. According to Matthew, they claimed Jesus said, "I am able to destroy the temple of God and to build it in three days." Mark adds that the witnesses said Jesus predicted that he would "destroy this temple that is made with hands and in three days build another not made with hands." The charge is more than Jesus would destroy a physical building, but that he would also eliminate temple worship, as it was known and replace it with a new and spiritual system of worship. These charges are similar to the words of Jesus in John 2:19, but misquoted and misinterpreted. However, it is true that Jesus stressed more the spiritual dynamics of worship more the outward aspects of worship in a physical place. Much of the testimony seems to have been inconclusive and contradictory to other testimony. However, early Christians were accused of having similar anti-temple sentiments. For example, in Acts 6:13-14, Stephen was also accused of speaking against the temple and predicting that Jesus would one day destroy the temple.

With the unsuccessful testimony of the witnesses against Jesus, the high priest called for Jesus to testify concerning himself. However, Jesus did not answer any of the charges that had been brought against him. Then the high priest urged Jesus to answer his question as to whether or not he was the Messiah, the Son of God. Each of the synoptic gospels present a different version of Jesus' answer.

1. Matthew 26:64: "Jesus said to him, 'You have said so.'"
2. Mark 14:62: "Jesus said, "I am.'"
3. Luke 22:67-68, 70: "He replied, 'If I tell you, you will not believe; and if I question you, you will not answer.' He said to them, 'You say that I am.'"

After this incriminating response, Jesus predicted that they would see the Son of Man coming with the clouds of heaven, presumably to judge the wicked and unfaithful. Apparently he intended for them to understand that whatever they did to him, one day, he would return as the victorious Son of Man and judge them, the very ones who were judging Jesus. Jesus' answer led the high priest to tear his garment and demand a verdict of guilty for blasphemy.

The denials of Peter (Matthew 26:69-75, Mark 14:66-72, Luke 22:54-62)

At the last supper, Jesus had predicted that Peter would deny him three times before the cock crowed. Matthew and Mark place all the denials of Peter together following the trial before Caiaphas. John places the first denial between the hearing before Annas and the trial before Caiaphas. The second and third seemed to have occurred during the trial. Peter's first denials occurred when a servant girl thought she recognized him as being an associate or disciple of Jesus. Peter's second denial came about from the pressure of another maid who claimed she saw him with Jesus. The third denial came about because Peter's obvious Galilean accent was detected. Since Jesus was from Galilee, a logical assumption would be that anyone near the trial who was from Galilee must have been a disciple of Jesus. As Jesus predicted, the cock crowed after the third denial. The expression "cock crowed" may not have been a reference to a bird call, but simply a designated time when there was a changing of the guards.

The official and formal meeting of the Sanhedrin in the early morning (Matthew 27:1-2, Mark 15:1, Luke 22:66-23:1)

According to Matthew and Mark the Sanhedrin met in the early morning following the night trials. The apparent purpose of this meeting was to formalize their verdict of condemnation of Jesus that informally had been decided at the night trials. Luke has combined the events of the night trial with the morning meeting as if it were one meeting. The clear decision of the council was to condemn Jesus as a blasphemer and to seek his death, as the Law so required.

The death of Judas (Matthew 27:3-10)

Matthew indicates that Judas repented for what he had done when he saw that Jesus had been condemned. This may mean that Judas never intended for Jesus to die. It may also mean that for the first time he truly realized the enormity of the evil he had committed, and so he repented. Matthew also records that Judas not only repented, but he also confessed his sin and sought to return the money. However, the priests refused to take back the money. Unwilling to keep the money, he decided to throw the money into the temple. Judas then hanged himself, apparently in deep remorse and feeling that he was beyond the pale of God's mercy. Perhaps he thought that the only thing he could do to absolve himself of his sin was to die. Judas' money was used by the priest to buy a field that would be used as a burial place for foreigners. The field was called "the Field of Blood."

Jesus' first hearing before Pilate (Matthew 27:11-14, March 15:2-5, Luke 23:2-5)

The Jewish council, upon condemning Jesus, decided to hand him over to Pontius Pilate for execution, since only Rome had that right. Luke records that the council brought three charges against Jesus before Pilate: "We found this man perverting our nation, forbidding us to pay taxes to the emperor, and says he himself is the Messiah, a king" (Luke 23:2). Essentially, the council took the heresy charges and turned them into political charges.

Pilate's initial interrogation led him to the conclusion that Jesus was innocent. However, the leaders continued to stress that Jesus had been a major agitator among the people in Galilee. Pilate then decided that Herod Antipas, governor of Galilee, should handle this case. As well as strengthening ties with Herod , Pilate may have hoped he wouldn't have to decide Jesus' guilt or innocence.

Jesus' hearing before Herod (Luke 23:6-16)

Luke states that Herod had wanted to see Jesus for some time. At one time, he thought Jesus was John the Baptist come back from the dead. Because Jesus had a reputation for being a miracle worker, he wanted to see Jesus perform some type of miracle. To his probable surprise and disappointment, Jesus said and did nothing. Nevertheless, Herod was not able to find anything incriminating against Jesus, so Herod decided to send Jesus back to Pilate for a final decision.

Jesus' second appearance before Pilate and final condemnation (Matthew 27:15-26, March 15:6-15, Luke 23:17-25)

The gospel of John records an extensive conversation between Pilate and Jesus. While Pilate did not find Jesus guilty of anything, the religious leaders continued to push for Jesus' death (John 18:33-19:12). Matthew states that Pilate's wife warned her husband about how he should "have nothing to do with this innocent man," for she had been dreaming about him (Matthew 27:19). Then, according to custom, Pilate offered to let one condemned prisoner free. The people could choose Barabbas or Jesus. Barabbas seems to have been a political activist and terrorist who was in prison for murder. Probably he enjoyed some popularity as a patriot for the independence of Judea. The name Barabbas means "Son of the Father."

There are some ancient manuscripts of the New Testament which give the full name as Jesus Barabbas or Jesus the Son of the Father. Most likely, Pilate thought the people would choose Jesus, and thus he could set him free as an act of political generosity. But the people were at least partially influenced by the religious leaders who selected Barabbas, and cried out for Jesus' crucifixion.

Pilate's decision to send Jesus to the cross is described as an act of political expediency. Matthew says that Pilate was afraid there might be a riot if he didn't agree to crucify Jesus. Mark says that Pilate wanted to satisfy the crowd. John adds that the crowd threatened Pilate that they would complain to the emperor that he was tolerating serious criminals (John 19:12). If the emperor believed the charges, Pilate would have been in serious political trouble. Despite all this, Pilate still could have prevented Jesus' death, but didn't because Jesus wasn't important enough for him to protect. The symbolic washing of his hands supposedly absolved Pilate of any moral or legal responsibility for this injustice. According to Matthew, the people willingly accepted this responsibility. Therefore, Jesus received his final condemnation from Pilate, and he was led away to be crucified.

Assessment of the trial of Jesus

According to the gospels, the Jewish phase of Jesus' trial violated either the rules or the spirit of the Jewish understanding of justice. The primary trial was held at night and apparently not publicly. Later laws required that capital trials must be held in the daytime hours. Since a verdict of guilty in a capital trial is a very serious matter, Jewish law later also required that the council must wait at least one day after the end of the trial to officially render the verdict. The gospels state that the decision of guilty was made almost immediately or after only a few hours interval during the morning session.

This trial used witnesses whose testimonies did not always agree with each other, and some of these witnesses were explicitly accused of being false. Against later rules, Jesus, the accused, was forced to testify concerning the charges, and his testimony was used against him with really no other collaborating evidence. In general, Jesus was treated as if already guilty, and the trial or hearing seems to have been almost a formality to legitimize the Jewish leaders' desire for his execution.

Pilate and the Roman courts seemed to have outwardly followed all the proper procedures. Pilate is described as acting clearly within the scope of the Roman Law on justice. On the surface, Pilate even seems to have had some concern for justice in that he initially sought to prevent an innocent man from being condemned to death. Like a competent Roman governor, he did not let himself get involved in local religious squabbles, but simply focused on the need for law and order.

Pilate's crime is that he seemed to have used his position and the justice system to further his political position. While he did not want to see an innocent man die, he even more did not want to see his political career end over such an apparently insignificant person as Jesus. He followed all the appropriate procedures. He even used this trial to score some political points with Herod. Thus, he sought justice, but not at the cost of his job. When it became clear that nothing would change the Sanhedrin's mind and that only by a politically risky executive decision would Jesus be free, Pilate gave in and thereby protected his position.

Chapter 23

The Crucifixion of Jesus

The flogging and mocking of Jesus (Matthew 27:26-31, Mark 15:15-20)

After Jesus was officially condemned by Pilate, he was handed over to soldiers to be flogged. Flogging was usually done with a whip made of several leather thongs, which were studded with sharpened pellets of lead, iron, and pieces of bone. A whip made this way could tear flesh from a person's body. In fact, many who were flogged often lost consciousness or became insane. After the flogging, the soldiers made sport of Jesus by dressing him with a scarlet robe, a crown of thorns, which was probably thrust on to his head, and a reed to serve as a scepter. They both spat on him and struck him with the reed. When they were through taunting him, they made him put on his own clothes and led him to be crucified.

The procession to Golgotha (Matthew 27:32, Mark 15:21, Luke 23:26-32)

Simon carries Jesus' cross

A typical processional party for execution consisted of the condemned criminal and four soldiers, probably two in front of the criminal and two in back. There may have been a herald walking in front of the group carrying a sign which contained the prisoner's name and the crime for which he was convicted. Often the procession would take the longest possible route through the busy streets of a city as a warning to others. As the prisoner would pass through the city, bystanders would often lash out or even goad the prisoner.

It is not certain exactly what it was Jesus was carrying--either the entire cross, or possibly the long base for the cross, or perhaps even the cross bar itself. Whatever it was, at some point on his fateful journey the exhausted and weakened Jesus had no more strength to carry his cross. So a certain Simon was summoned to carry Jesus' cross the rest of the way to the place of execution. Simon was from the North African city of Cyrene. The fact that Simon was in Jerusalem at Passover time suggests that he was Jewish. However, he also may have been African or an African Jew through conversion, something like the Ethiopian Eunuch of Acts 8. Mark mentions that Simon was the father of Alexander and Rufus, which implies that Alexander and Rufus were known by the Christian community to whom Mark had originally penned this gospel. Thus, Simon may have been a disciple of Jesus who later became a Christian. Paul greets a Rufus in Romans 16:3, and it is generally believed that Mark was originally written in Rome.

Jesus' words to the wailing women (Luke 23:26-31)

Jesus' procession attracted a large crowd of curious onlookers. Within the crowd were women who were probably regular funeral or death march mourners. When Jesus came near to these women, he spoke words of warning and concern for them. He warned that a worse time was coming--a time when childlessness becomes a blessing and people will desire to hide.

He warned that if his crucifixion was terrible, certainly future events will be even worse. Most likely he was referring to the destruction of Jerusalem.

The Crucifixion (Matthew 27:33-44, Mark 15:22-32, Luke 23:33-43)

"They crucified him"

Mark states that Jesus was crucified at 9:00 a.m. Someone offered Jesus wine mixed with gall, apparently to deaden the pain, but he refused to take it. He must have wanted to have his complete faculties as he went through this horrible experience. The gospels mention the crucifixion in a very matter-of-fact way, with no elaboration or gruesome details, although it was clearly a most humiliating and horrible form of execution. The clinical nature and horror of Jesus' death was of less importance than the meaning of it for Christians. The soldiers gambled for his clothes. An inscription was also placed over Jesus' head in three languages giving his name and the crime for which he was being executed. No doubt this served as an added warning against anyone else who would dare challenge the authority of Rome. Jesus was crucified between two criminals.

The words of Jesus on the cross

Taken together, the four gospels contain seven sayings or words of Jesus while on the cross. No one gospel contains all seven and some of the sayings only appear in one of the gospels. While the exact order of the sayings cannot be determined with certainty, the following is the discussion of the traditional order of these sayings.

Saying 1: *"Father, forgive them; for they do not know what they are doing."* (Luke 23:34) While the text does not explicitly indicate when Jesus said this, it may be that he said this either as they were crucifying him or immediately after they completed nailing him to the cross. Jesus may have been praying explicitly for the soldiers or for everyone who had a part in his crucifixion.

Saying 2*: "Truly I tell you, today you will be with me in Paradise."* (Luke 23: 43) These words were said to the thief on the cross who apparently had repented and expressed faith in Jesus. Luke recorded this at the conclusion of the section in which Jesus had been mocked and scoffed at. According to Matthew and Mark, many of the observers taunted him concerning his claim to be the Son of God. For Matthew the taunts were reminiscent of Jesus' temptation in the wilderness: "If you are the Son of God, come down from the cross." Perhaps, the writer understood that even at this late hour, Satan was tempting Jesus to choose another path to greatness. The sarcastic jeers challenged Jesus to prove himself by coming down from the cross or calling on God for deliverance. Everyone joined in with the taunts, including the soldiers and even the other two condemned prisoners. But Luke records that one of the prisoners began to rebuke his fellow prisoner. He said that while they were truly deserving of the punishment Jesus was not. Then he asked Jesus for mercy, and in so doing revealed his own faith. He was the only one who publicly supported Jesus at that time.

Saying 3*: "Woman, here is your son." Then he said to the disciple, "Here is your mother."* (John 19:26-27). This third statement comes from the gospel of John and reveals his concern for his mother while at the point of death.

Saying 4*: "My God, my God, why have you forsaken me?"* (Matthew 27:46, Mark 15:34) Both Matthew and Mark give the Aramaic version of this cry of anguish. The text records that beginning at noon, the sky was entirely covered in darkness until about 3:00 p.m. Then Jesus uttered these words of despair, a direct quote from Psalm 22:1. That particular psalm contains many verses which seem to clearly point toward the crucifixion, yet the motivation of Jesus to quote these words is not easy to determine. A common theory is that Jesus was crying out that God had forsaken him because he was carrying the sins of the world on him, and thus was repugnant to the Father's eyes. Only at the resurrection was Jesus' relation with God restored. A second interpretation suggests that these words were simply a cry of despair by a human who was facing his own imminent death. He was afraid and in a panic. Finally, it should be noted that Psalm 22 ends in a song of triumph because God did in fact hear the psalmist's cry and saw his plight. If Psalm 22 is pointing to the death of Jesus, perhaps it is telling the reader that God never abandons his faithful people, no matter how terrible the circumstances.

Saying 5: *"I am thirsty"* (John 19:28) These words may have been a sign that his death was very near, and the fact that he was given a drink was an act of mercy. John also notes that Jesus said this after he knew that everything had been accomplished, so this saying of Jesus was another deliberate step in Jesus' conscious effort to complete this final work that God gave him to do.

Saying 6: *"It is finished"* (John 19:30) This was a declaration by Jesus that he had, in fact, completed the mission which God had given him. Thus, these are not words of defeat but of victory.

Saying 7: *"Father, into your hands I commend my spirit."* (Luke 23:46) Matthew, Mark and Luke all state that Jesus gave a loud cry moments before his death. Luke, however, records that this final cry was his final prayer. These words are a quotation from Psalm 31:5. Tradition claims that these words became a type of child's lullaby, which a child might say prior to going to sleep. Perhaps the first prayer, maybe the first Bible verse Jesus ever learned and said, became his last. This verse expresses the type of complete trust one can enjoy with God. With these words, Jesus died in peace.

Accompanying events

When Jesus died, Matthew and Mark record that the temple curtain was torn in two. This was no doubt symbolic of the breaking of barriers between God and humankind through the Cross. Matthew mentions that many bodies of the saints who had died were raised. Now the term "saints" may refer to heroes in Israel's past. Apparently, there were no appearances of these raised saints until after the resurrection of Jesus. However, the entire event is mysterious and is described as a type of prelude to the final resurrection and last judgment. All three synoptic gospels record the conclusion of the centurion who was at the cross. According to Luke, he concluded that Jesus must be innocent, but Matthew and Mark testify that the centurion said that Jesus was God's Son. Matthew and Mark's version can mean that the soldier came to faith in Jesus or that he was a godly man, which is similar to Luke's version that he was innocent. Most likely the soldier was merely declaring his admiration of Jesus as a good, pious and innocent man. Finally, Luke suggests that the crowd reacted as if they deeply regretted what had happened.

The burial of Jesus (Matthew 27:57-61, Mark 15:42-47, Luke 23:50-56)

John 19:31-37 records that the Jews requested from Pilate that the bodies be removed from the crosses in order that the sabbath might no be defiled. This would require the removal of the bodies before 6 p.m. They even requested that they break the legs of anyone who might still be alive. The soldiers arrived and broke the legs of the two thieves, but found Jesus already dead. His death was further confirmed when a soldier pierced his side, out of which came both blood and water.

Joseph of Arimathea requested the body of Jesus for burial. John described him as a secret disciple of Jesus. He was a member of the Sanhedrin (Council), but had not agreed to the council's plan to kill Jesus. When Pilate got confirmation of Jesus' death, he granted Joseph's request. John 19:39-40 also records that Joseph was assisted by Nicodemus, another member of the council, who may have been a secret disciple. Mary Magdalene along with other women went to the place where Jesus was buried so that they would know where to find his body and anoint Jesus with prepared spices and ointments as a last act of honor. Meanwhile, according to Matthew, the Jewish leaders received permission to seal and guard Jesus' tomb in order to prevent anyone from stealing the body and then falsely claim that he had been raised from the dead (Matthew 27:62-66).

Chapter 24

The Resurrection and Ascension of Jesus

Introduction

The story of the resurrection of Jesus centers around two major claims: (1) the tomb of Jesus was empty; and (2) there were many claims of appearances of the risen Jesus. The following survey of the resurrection story will follow these two points. Whenever a person studies the gospels' account of the resurrection of Jesus, he or she will notice both the remarkable similarity and dissimilarity in content among the gospel records. In fact, some scholars have argued that, in certain parts of the resurrection story, the four gospels are hopelessly irreconcilable. While such skepticism is not necessary, we must realize that harmonization of the four gospel accounts is a very difficult task. Therefore, any sequencing of events are based on opinion and not absolute evidence. The following is the outline of events which, in my opinion, is most likely the closest to what actually happened on Resurrection Day and afterwards.

1. The discovery of the empty tomb by the women.
2. The report of the women to the disciples.
3. The investigation of the tomb by Peter and the other disciples.

4. The appearance of the risen Jesus to the women (This includes the appearance of Jesus to Mary Magdalene. It is difficult to determine if there were one or two appearances to women.)
5. The appearance of the risen Jesus to the disciples on the way to Emmaus.
6. The appearance of the risen Jesus to the disciples in the closed room.
7. The appearance of the risen Jesus to the disciples, especially Thomas, in the house one week later.
8. The appearance of the risen Jesus to the disciples on the mountain in Galilee.
9. The appearance of the risen Jesus to the disciples at the sea of Galilee
10. The appearances of the risen Jesus during a 40-day period.
11. The appearance of the risen Jesus to Saul of Tarsus, later known as Paul.

The discovery of the empty tomb (Matthew 28:1-10, Mark 16:1-8, Luke 24:1-12)

The gospels state that on the first day of the week Mary Magdalene and other women went to the tomb to anoint the body of Jesus. When they arrived, they found the stone had been rolled away from the tomb and the tomb empty. Mark records that the women had been discussing who would roll away the stone from the tomb. When they arrived, they discovered that the stone had been rolled away. Matthew notes that there was a great earthquake and an angel from heaven came down and rolled away the stone from the tomb. When the guards saw the angels, they became overwhelmed with fear. At this point, Matthew and Mark state that the angel declared to the women that Jesus had been raised from the dead and that they were to go and tell the disciples that he would meet them in Galilee. Luke added that the angels (he mentioned that there were two men dressed in dazzling apparel) reminded them that when he was still with them in Galilee, Jesus had told them he would die and be raised.

The account in John 20:1-2 is different from the synoptics. John records that Mary Magdalene, upon seeing the empty tomb, immediately reported to the disciples that someone had stolen the body of Jesus. Similarly, Luke records that Mary and the others told the apostles of having seen the risen Jesus. Luke adds that their report had to do with having seen angels and hearing reports that Jesus had been raised from the dead. Yet, according to John, Mary believed in Jesus' resurrection only after she visited the tomb a second time. During that visit Mary talked with the angels and finally saw the risen Jesus. Perhaps John narrows his focus on Mary, while the other accounts represents an abbreviation and combination of the material in John.

After the women had reported to the apostles, Luke states Peter and possibly others saw the empty tomb, but could not account for it, so they were just as confused as before. Similarly, John records that Peter and the Beloved Disciple went to the tomb and saw the burial clothes laying neatly. Thus, while the evidence did not seem to support that there had been grave robbers at Jesus' tomb, they seemed very confused.

The appearances of the risen Jesus

The appearance of the risen Jesus to the women (Matthew 28:8-10)

According to Matthew, the women left the tomb of Jesus to report to the apostles as the angel had instructed. As they were traveling, Jesus appeared to them. In joyful reaction to this appearance, the women took hold of Jesus and worshipped him. Jesus then encouraged them and repeated the instructions that had been given by the angel. John records an appearance of Jesus to Mary Magdalene, presumably alone (John 20:11-18). After she gave her initial report to the apostles concerning the empty tomb, Mary returned to the tomb of Jesus to weep for him. At that time, she met two angels standing by the place where Jesus' body had been, and they asked her why she was weeping. Then she saw Jesus, though she did not recognize him. Only after he spoke her name did she know who he was. Jesus instructed her to go and tell his disciples that he was alive and soon would ascend to the Father. She then went to the apostles and declared that she had seen the Lord.

The bribing of the soldiers (Matthew 28:11-15)

The soldiers who had stood guard at the tomb of Jesus returned to the city and reported to the chief priests what had happened. That may have included the descending of the angel, the rolling away of the stone, the resurrection of Jesus, and the empty tomb. For fear that their story might spread throughout the city, the religious leaders offered a large sum of money to the soldiers to state that the disciples had stolen the body; the soldiers agreed. Matthew notes that the Jews were still using this explanation for the empty tomb even at the time of the writing of that gospel.

The appearance of the risen Jesus to the disciples on the road to Emmaus (Luke 24:13-35)

Luke records that two disciples, one named Cleopas, were traveling by foot to the village of Emmaus when they came upon a stranger who joined them. The text indicates that the stranger was Jesus, though they did not recognize him. As these men were discussing the events of the past few days, the stranger asked what they were talking about. Surprised at his apparent ignorance, they proceeded to review all the events surrounding Jesus of Nazareth, especially his death, burial, and strange events in the aftermath. Then Jesus began to instruct them in the truth that everything that had taken place was part of God's will and prophesied in Scripture. When they arrived in Emmaus, they asked Jesus to stay for dinner; he consented. Then, while at the table, he took the bread, blessed it and broke it. At that moment, Luke states that the disciples' eyes were opened, and they recognized him as Jesus. He then vanished from their sight. Immediately, they returned to Jerusalem and found the place where the rest of the disciples were staying. They reported what had happened to them. In response, the group agreed that Jesus had been raised and that he had appeared to Simon Peter.

The appearance of the risen Jesus to the disciples in Jerusalem (Luke 24:36-49)

As the group of disciples were discussing these recent events, Jesus suddenly appeared to them. At first the disciples were terrified, but Jesus reassured them that it was he, and calmed their fears. He invited them to investigate his body, hands, and feet to convince themselves that this was no illusion. He even ate broiled fish in front of them. Following that he gave them a commission to preach a message of repentance and forgiveness of sins in Jesus' name to all nations. In order to accomplish this great work, he promised to give them power from on high, i.e., the Holy Spirit. Most likely the appearance of Jesus in John 20:19-25 is the same event. John tells the reader that Thomas was absent at that meeting. One week later, John records that Jesus again appeared to the disciples but this time with Thomas present. Jesus invited Thomas, who had been skeptical of Jesus' resurrection, to examine him (even his wounds) in order to see that this was really Jesus.

The appearance of the risen Jesus on the mountain top in Galilee (Matthew 28:16-20)

At this meeting, Jesus stressed that all authority had been given to him. He also commissioned his disciples to make disciples of all nations. This disciplining process would involve two tasks, baptism and teaching. He also promised that he would be with the Church to the end of time. This may have been the same event which Paul mentioned in I Corinthians 15:6, that more than 500 people at one time saw him alive.

The appearance of the risen Jesus to the disciples near the Sea of Galilee (John 21)

This resurrection appearance of Jesus has been difficult for scholars to assess. Some have questioned this story's authenticity since it is remarkably similar to the story of a miraculous catch of fish in Luke 5 when Jesus called men to be his disciples and told them he would make them become fishers of men. Others have pointed out that John 21 is clearly an appendix to the fourth gospel and was not a part of the original plan of the gospel. Since it was probably added by a disciple of John's, that might raise some doubt concerning its genuineness. Still others who have accepted this story as true find it extremely difficult to chronologically place it. The main point of the story is that Peter was spiritually restored to Jesus. As Peter denied Jesus three times, so here Jesus asked Peter to affirm his love for him three times.

The ascension of Christ (Luke 24:50-53)

In his account of the resurrection, Luke states that while Jesus was blessing the disciples with lifted hands he was carried up into heaven. Luke expands on this story in Acts 1:11. Luke wrote that a cloud took Jesus out of the sight of the disciples. The significance of the ascension was not in the direction Jesus went but the exalted state Jesus was granted due to his faithfulness. The ancient world believed in a flat earth, with a dome shaped sky and a dark underworld beneath the surface of the earth. With contemporary world's understanding of the universe, it is not necessary to believe that when Jesus went into heaven he simply traveled up above the earth until he arrived. Rather, Jesus' ascension was more of a symbol of his exaltedness. God made Jesus sit at the right hand of the majesty on high and declared him to be Lord and Christ with power.

Epilogue

Mark's longer resurrection account

While many Bibles contain the passage of Mark 16:9-20, the majority of the best Greek New Testament manuscripts do not contain this. Thus, most scholars would characterize this passage as a later addition, probably added by a scribe. Then, too, nothing in this text sheds any light to the story of the resurrection and ascension of Jesus.

Paul's testimony to Jesus' resurrection

Paul said in I Corinthians 15:8 Jesus appeared to him "last of all." The book of Acts contains three accounts of Paul's witness to the risen Jesus: Acts 9:1-22, 22:4-16, and 26:9-18. The first is the author's account, and the last two are Paul's testimony of the same incident to two different audiences. In Galatians 1:16, Paul wrote that God revealed His son to him. This event had a life changing effect on Paul. He stated that the resurrection appearance of Jesus was what led him to become a Christian and helped him understand the grace of God in his life (1 Corinthians 15:9-10). Later, church tradition testified that the appearances of the risen Christ ceased after his appearance to Paul, some 18 months after the first Easter.

The historicity of the resurrection of Jesus

From the earliest days of Christianity, many people have rejected the resurrection of Jesus as too impossible to believe. Despite what some have described as fairly early and consistent evidence, many remained unconvinced. In response to the Christian claims, alternative explanations have been suggested as the best explanation of the evidence. Some of these alternative suggestions are: (1) the disciples stole the body of Jesus; (2) the women went to the wrong tomb; (3) the swoon theory--Jesus did not really die but merely appeared to be and then recovered (it should be noted that this theory flies in the face of all the available evidence both biblical and non-biblical, Christian or non-Christian); (4) the resurrection story is a nice myth but unhistorical, completely fabricated by the disciples; and (5) the disciples experienced psychological illusions.

In order to assess the strength of any suggested theory, one must be able to assess how well a given theory accounts for the evidence or data. The following is the evidence or data one must account for: (1) the tomb of Jesus was empty; (2) many people claimed to have seen the risen Jesus; (3) the cowardly apostles were radically changed and became people of boldness and courage only one month after the crucifixion; (4) the small, undermanned, and underfinanced congregations of Christians grew rapidly despite all the obstacles they had to undergo; and (5) Saul of Tarsus, a persecutor of the Church, was remarkably changed to become a follower of Christ, even an ardent and committed apostle. In my opinion, the only theory which best explains the evidence is that Jesus in fact did rise from the dead. If it is true that Jesus of Nazareth was raised from the dead, then how should one consider this Jesus? For Paul, the resurrection was critical for a true understanding of Jesus. In the opening verses of his letter to the Christians in Rome, Paul set forth in summary fashion his belief concerning Jesus in light of the resurrection:

> "Paul, a servant of Jesus Christ, called to be an apostle, set apart for the gospel of God, which he promised beforehand through his prophets in the holy scriptures, the gospel concerning his Son, who was descended from David according to the flesh and was declared to be the Son of God with power according to the spirit of holiness by resurrection from the dead, Jesus Christ our Lord" (Romans 1:1-4).

Who is this Jesus?

The story of Jesus has been an interesting and compelling one for many people. From the beginning of Christianity, many have believed Jesus was more than simply a human being. According to the book of Acts, the earliest sermons proclaimed that Jesus was a man through whom God demonstrated his miraculous power, who was raised from the dead by God, and was subsequently exalted to the position of Lord and Messiah (Acts 2:22-36). Paul confessed that "for us there is one God, the Father, from whom are all things and for whom we exist, and one Lord, Jesus Christ, through whom are all things and through whom we exist." (1 Corinthians 8:6). In another letter Paul quoted from an early Christian hymn which proclaim:

> Who, though he was in the form of God,
>   did not regard equality with God
>   as something to be exploited,
> but emptied himself,
>   taking the form of a slave,
>   being born in human likeness.

And being found in human form,
    he humbled himself
    and became obedient to the
        point of death—
    even death on a cross.
Therefore God also highly exalted him
    and gave him the name
    that is above every name,
so that at the name of Jesus
    every knee should bend,
    in heaven and on earth and under the earth,
and every tongue should confess
    that Jesus Christ is Lord,
    to the glory of God the Father. (Philippians 2:6-11)

According to 1 Peter, Jesus is our true example:

> For to this you have been called, because Christ also suffered for you, leaving you an example, so that you should follow in his steps.
>
> "He committed no sin, and no deceit was found in his mouth."
>
> When he was abused, he did not return abuse; when he suffered, he did not threaten; but he entrusted himself to the one who judges justly. He himself bore our sins in his body on the cross, so that, free from sins, we might live for righteousness; by his wounds you have been healed. For you were going astray like sheep, but now you have returned to the shepherd and guardian of your souls. (1 Peter 2:21-25)

The unknown writer of Hebrews describes Jesus as greater than angels, Moses, and a greater high priest than the priesthood in Israel. More than that, Jesus was the Son "through whom he [God] also created the worlds. He is the reflection of God's glory and the exact imprint of God's very being, and he sustains all things by his powerful word" (Hebrews 1:2b-3a). Similarly, the gospel of John opens with declaring that Jesus was the eternal Word who had not only existed with God and was God (shared God's divine nature), but was also the one through whom God created all things. (John 1:1-4). The writer of Revelation even declares Jesus to be "Lord of lords and King of kings." (Revelation 17:14b)

The question and mystery surrounding the nature of Jesus has continued throughout the centuries. People have asked, "How can Jesus be both divine and human? Isn't that like mixing oil and water?" Others have wondered how they can know Jesus is the Son of God. For centuries, the greatest religious minds have attempted to answer these and other questions. From these great thinkers have merged some of the most profound concepts of God and Jesus in the form of creeds and books on theology. However, when one reads the New Testament, one encounters confessions, hymns of faith, and pastoral instruction, yet little in speculative theology. In contrast to many of the great religious minds of the last two centuries, the first Christians believed they experienced God in community. They heard the gospel of God's love as seen in the life, words and death of Jesus, accepted it, and in fellowship with others experienced what they believed was the living Jesus in their lives. As a result they understood that being a Christian was more than simply believing in Jesus, but it meant living for and like Jesus. His mission is now the mission of the Christian community. That is why Paul described the Church as the body of Christ, for through the life and work of the Church, Jesus continues to carry out his ministry.

Selected Bibliography

Barclay, William. *The Mind of Christ*. New York: Harper and Row, 1960.

Beare, Francis W. *The Earliest Records of Jesus*. Nashville: Abingdon, 1963.

Brown, Raymond. *The Birth of the Messiah*. updated edition. NY: Doubleday, 1993.

Brown, Raymond. *The Death of the Messiah*. 2 Volumes. NY: Doubleday, 1994.

Connick, C. Milo. *Jesus, the Man, the Mission and the Message*. Englewood Cliffs, NJ: Prentice Hall, 1974.

Cranfield, C. E. B. *The Gospel According to Mark*. London: Cambridge University Press, 1966.

Dodd, C. H. *The Parables of the Kingdom*. NY: Scribners, 1961.

Edersheim, Alfred. *The Life and Times of Jesus the Messiah*. Grand Rapids, Mich: Eerdmanns, Reprint 1976.

Fitzmyer, Joseph. *The Gospel According to Luke*. Vol. 1. NY: Doubleday, 1981.

Fitzmyer, Joseph. *The Gospel According to Luke*. Vol 2. NY: Doubleday, 1985.

Green, Joel B., McKnight, Scot, and Marshall, I. Howard, eds. *Dictionary of Jesus and the Gospel*. Downers Grove, Ill: InterVarsity Press, 1992.

Guelich, Robert. *The Sermon on the Mount.* Waco, Tex: Word, 1982.

Harrison, Everett. *A Short Life of Christ.* Grand Rapids, Mich: Eerdmans, 1968.

Hill, David. *Matthew.* Grand Rapids, Mich: Eerdmans, 1981.

Jeremias, Joachim. *The Parables of Jesus.* NY: Scribners, 1972.

Johnson, Luke Timothy. *The Gospel According to Luke.* Collegeville, Minn: Liturgical Press, 1991.

Kee, Howard Clark. *Jesus in History: An Approach to the Study of the Gospels.* NY: HBJ College and School Div, 1996.

Klausner, Joseph. *Jesus of Nazareth.* Trans. Herbert Danby. NY: MacMillan and Co. 1944.

Lane, William. *The Gospel According to Mark.* Grand Rapids, Mich: Eerdmans, 1974.

Machen, J.Gresham. *The Virgin Birth of Christ.* Grand Rapids, Mich: Baker Books, Reprint 1967.

Manson, T. W. *The Sayings of Jesus.* Grand Rapids, Mich: Eerdmans, 1979.

Meier, John P. *A Marginal Jew: Rethinking the Historical Jesus.* Vol. 1 NY: Doubleday, 1991.

Meier, John P. *A Marginal Jew: Rethinking the Historical Jesus.* Vol. 2. NY: Doubleday, 1994.

Summers, Ray. *The Secret Sayings of the Living Jesus.* Waco, Tex: Word, 1968.

Tatum, W. Barnes. *In Quest of Jesus.* Nashville: Abingdon, 1999.

Taylor, Vincent. *The Formation of the Gospel.* NY: Macmillan, 1933.

Van Voorst, Robert E. *Jesus Outside the New Testament: An Introduction to the Ancient Evidence.* Grand Rapids, Mich: Eerdmans, 2000.

Whitson, William, Trans. *The New Complete Works of Josephus.* Grand Rapids, Mich: Kregel, 1999.

Wright, N. T. *Jesus and the Victory of God.* Minneapolis, Minn: Fortress, 1996.

Lightning Source UK Ltd.
Milton Keynes UK
UKOW06f1405290716

279523UK00001B/207/P

9 781597 526067